TOM OF TWOFOLD BAY

TOM OF TWOFOLD BAY

Nigel Clayton

First published in Australia by Meni Publishing and Binding in
2008

Copyright © Nigel Clayton t/as Meni Publishing and Binding,
2008, 2015

Printed by CreateSpace, an Amazon.com Company.

Nigel Clayton
Tom of Twofold Bay, Second Edition.
ISBN 978 0 9802 985 3 6

1. Clayton, Nigel, 1963- . 2. Killer whale - New South Wales -
Twofold Bay - Fiction. 3. Whaling - New South Wales - Twofold
Bay - Fiction. I. Title.

A823.4

Other Titles by this Author

The Long Road to Rwanda
Colonies of Earth
Fall of the Inca Empire
Inca Myths and Way of Life
The Templar: and the City of God
The Templar: and the Temple of Káros
The Templar: and the Cross of Christ
Underworld
Spacescape
Space Opera – Heaven and Hell
Tom of Twofold Bay
The Zuytdorp Survivors
Afghan
Afghan: The Script
Chivalry
The Caves of Hiroshima
Scourge
The Cure
Amazon
Furious George
This Pestilence, Bergen-Belsen
Templar, Assassination, Trial & Torture
Underworld
When the Virgin Falls
Kibeho: Original Script
The Kibeho Massacre: As It Happened
Non, Je Ne Regrette Rien - No, I (We) Have No Regrets
The Matter with Karen Mitchell

About the Author

Nigel joined the Australian Army in 1980 at age 17yrs and 2 months, and after completing training at Kapooka was whisked away to the School of Infantry, Singleton, New South Wales, Australia.

He served in the Infantry until injury forced a medical discharge upon him in 1996, after having served in Southeast Asia, 1982; PNG (with the AATPT), in 1990: during the Bougainville Crisis; and in Rwanda, 1995: known world-wide for the Kibeho Massacre which occurred on April 22nd of that year.

Serving in PNG was a major highlight within his career.

He was married in 1999 and has two children.

IMPORTANT NOTE:

Some of the evidence and general information concerning Typee and Jackson, during cross-examination, appears misconstrued and vastly different, as does other aspects of this work. I have put forward the history of the bay as interpreted, being more inclined to favour Tom Mead's point of view, as recorded by the interview of witnesses.

This is a work of Historical-Fiction and should not be used as a source on which to base the history of Eden. Whaling events over the years have been pruned and extended to bring to light the charismatic behaviour of the interaction between man and killer whale as best as possible; I apologise if I have dealt truth an injustice by doing so.

This is the story of the killer whales of Eden.

FAST FISH

A harpoon entering the body of a whale did not kill it; it was meant only as a means by which to secure the line and maintain a measure of control over the whale whilst lancing took place and the animal then killed; this might take some time and some number of lances. It was therefore not surprising to see that a rule was employed by which means a crew could announce quite categorically that 'it' owned the right to the whale in which its harpoon was attached; it went something like this: where the harpoon shall remain in the fish so struck, and a line or boat shall be attached thereto and continue in the power of the striker or headsman, such whale shall be deemed a fast fish, and although struck by any secondary or subsequent harpoon shall be the property of the first striker or headsman only.

COMMON BOAT LAYOUT

Nine metres long and pointed at both ends with a sag in the middle, wide in breadth around where the centre thwart lay, each differing slightly but built objectively the same, dependant on the maker. There was planking across the first 1.5 metres of the stern where the loggerhead could be found, a short post where line was checked, it being drenched with buckets of water during hectic times when whales took off with the line attached, the friction of which was quite easily capable of seeing the loggerhead burst into flames. Tubs which contained the line (fed through the loggerhead) were found between the middle and aft thwarts, depending on the headsman, 200 fathoms of line (manila rope) to each. The line was fed through the loggerhead and continued on through a niche in the bow, under an iron bar and then back over it to the harpoon, where it was attached securely. A typical boat would have anywhere from 5-8 oarsman, the number most favoured being that which allowed for an equal number of oarsman to be positioned either side of the boat once the battle against a whale was commenced, a number derived upon by the headsman.

From the bow the following positions were normally filled: harpooner, bow-oarsman, midship-oarsman, tub-oarsman, after-oarsman, headsman (at the stern); each seated upon his own thwart. The headsman was responsible for exchanging places with the harpooner once delivery of weapon had been secured within the beast, the harpooner responsible for securing 'fast fish'. The headsman, once having exchanged places with the harpooner, would then deliver as many lances as was required to fulfil his duty. The harpooner now controlled the sweep (steering oar) with great precision, it being 6.7-8.2 metres in length.

THE FAMILY TREE

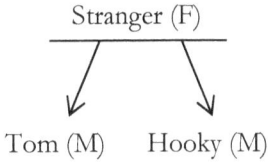

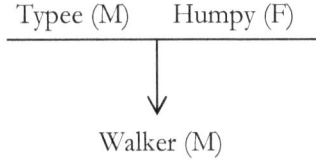

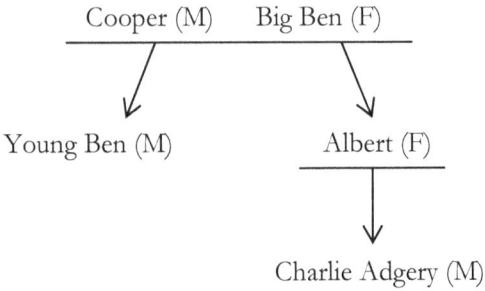

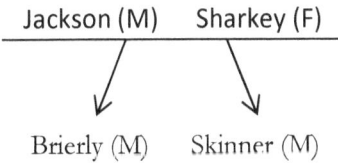

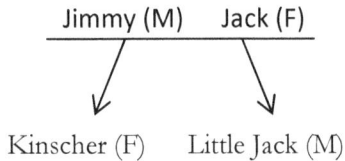

Stranger (F)

→ Tom (M) Hooky (M)

Typee (M) Humpy (F)

→ Walker (M)

Cooper (M) Big Ben (F)

→ Young Ben (M) Albert (F)

→ Charlie Adgery (M)

Jackson (M) Sharkey (F)

→ Brierly (M) Skinner (M)

Jimmy (M) Jack (F)

→ Kinscher (F) Little Jack (M)

PROLOGUE
GENERAL INFORMATION

Killer whales; the orca; they are black and white dolphins, mammals of the sea, warm-blooded creatures which are at the top of the food chain for the territory that they hold within their power, man being its only predator. Their upper and dorsal surface is black and their lower, ventral surface and the face (left and right sides), are white with a saddle patch upon their backs just behind the dorsal. Its light coloured under belly blends with the light of the surface, and prey from above are confused by the killer's darker upside. Camouflage has hence played an important role. A head on attack from a killer, whether speedily or more relaxed, can easily be confused as nothing more than shifting shadows, for the blazes upon its head in contrast to dark upper and light under can betray the mental deciphering of a hunter on the approach, a salmon falling easy victim, moving too late to avoid the menacing jaws as the killer closes its mouth over another meal.

Their dorsal fins literally tower above the surface of the sea, standing 1.8 metres tall in the case of an adult, where the male displays the most easily viewed of its signatures, and the female displays a shorter and more crescent shaped dorsal: similar to younger killers of adolescence or younger. It rekindles the melody of 'ebony and ivory' for it is black with patches of white upon its body, to break up its shape and threatening presence, so that other mammals and fish of the sea are drawn into a sense of false security when one swims near. It also has a distinctive pigmentation behind the dorsal, a patch noteworthy for its ability to aid in identification from one member and the next.

The tail flukes have no skeletal support but are more fibrous, the propulsion attained from powerful movement of the tail stock (or caudal peduncle). Their eyes are suited to both sea and air, killer whales lifting their heads out of the water to spy on their surrounds, to take in the beauty of the scenery around, and in the case of Twofold Bay, to look at those figures of flesh and bone that stand tall in little boats with harpoon and lances in hand. Yes indeed, sight plays a major role in the killer's day to day life, it being as good above the waves as it is below, but sound is a more important quality that it beholds, for sound is its tool of manipulation and strategy whereby food is placed before them like dinner upon a plate.

Of all the mammals of the sea they are the most travelled, the most widely distributed across the waters of the earth, the only significant winner in regards to travel being man, and although widely versed with the oceans of the world it tends to stay clear of the mid-Pacific, mid-Atlantic and mid-Indian Oceans, for no other discernible reason other than the fact that it endeavours, through all its daily rituals, to preserve energy and feast on flesh, whether it be the tongue of a baleen or the rump of a porpoise. Due to such reasons it is understandable that the highest concentration of killer whales can be found along the latitudes of both hemispheres where the temperature is more suitable for energy preservation and close to the coastlines where fertility in life plays a large role in sustaining a leisurely and measurable existence.

With its mouth of teeth, torpedo-shaped body and sheer size, it can outplay, out manoeuvre, chase down and intercept even the most noblest of other species of dolphin. The killer is extremely intelligent with a brain that dwarfs a man's. The killer's brain is three times the size of a man's, but size does not indicate a superior intelligence but more of an ability to undertake daily choirs with fuller understanding, where feelings of loneliness and despair can also be felt. But most of all the brain can decipher incoming sounds and piece together an intelligible communicative idea or action.

The killer can be classified into three main groups, each group depicting their general displays of behaviour and feeding. Killers live in a matriarch society whereby there is a strong bond between mothers, daughter, and granddaughters. This is the strength of any structured group comprising any number of animals, be it 'resident', 'transient', or 'offshore'.

In regards to the 'resident', the dispersal of individuals from the group does not occur; not whilst the mother is alive in any case. Groups are very large groups, pods of several dozen related killers, feeding exclusively on fish. Made up of a mother, and her sons and daughters of 3-10 killers, each contributes to the group of several dozen animals per pod (as a whole) via its matrilineal binding, up to several hundred individual animals becoming evident in its community. Matrilineal groups within a pod are created on equal terms where the size of any given pod is stretched to the limit, command and structure forming break-away groups of the same, or similar, matriarch society, known as sub-pods. Vocal strategies within a sub-pod are used extensively and remain throughout their lives, such repertoire of dialect being shared to a degree by other sub-pods within the pod and/or drawn from the pod in question.

Sub-pods can be looked upon as a 'constant' in a killer's society and remain steadfast for the entire life of the matriarch at least, and a killer will not usually defect from one sub-pod to another sub-pod, but smaller extensions of such a pod/sub-pods can be created from the larger. Pods also contained killers that shared, unequivocally, their complex mannerism of social and vocal range of communication, including their specific and unique language – call it accent or basic understanding of a different dialect.

The 'transient' are less social than 'resident' and travel in smaller groups of six or less, mainly feeding on sea lions, seals, porpoises and sea mammals. The 'offshore' usually constitutes a large group of 30-60 animals and they prefer open waters and feed mainly on fish, including salmon. Predatory habits are therefore harnessed in respect to each group and are good reason why other sources of food are not exploited.

Taste for food is as variable as the variety, although many areas where killer whales have grown accustom, do tend to spend a vast majority of their life feeding upon distinctive forms of prey. The world is a large surface area which provides many staples, some coastlines offering sea lions, seals, porpoises and dolphins; others may tend to feast on the fruits which are offered seasonally, such as salmon and other small fish like herring, even squid and seabirds. The Arctic offers penguins, humpbacks and seals, as does the Antarctic, not to mention more tropical areas where dugongs, turtles and manatees make a great meal. Where whales are concerned, in particular their migratory range and location, it isn't hard to understand how pods of killer whale can follow and maintain a full belly of humpback flesh along any of the world's coastlines which extend up from the Antarctic, one such migration route taking whales along the east coast of Australia and bypassing Twofold Bay, and in some cases with the intention for a frolic within the deep bay. For an orca to maintain a reasonable source of energy it must consume around four percent of its body weight per day, or starve and go by the way of death's door.

To secure food it must act with constant stealth until such a time that an order is given to move in for the kill, for this reason above all else the killer spends around 95 percent of its life under the waves and out of view, stalking its prey like the predator it is, using its physical and mental attributes as best it can to suffocate the source of its temptation in order to fill its quota for the day. But lack of food isn't the only killer of the orca for man also plays his hand in its demise. The cruel and efficient whaling programmes pursued in the past have seen to it that many of those that choose to feed off baleen whales have had their dinner plates cleaned for them and by the decreasing numbers of baleen whale available comes the inability to feed as required, hence a drop in the population of the killer which is continuing at an alarming rate – this also includes the sperm whale population which was decimated in years past.

When food becomes scarce the killer will draw energy sources from its high-calorie reserves of blubber, its huge bulk serving as a means to survive. Where weeks without food can turn into months the killer is able to hold back death, but age, whether young or old, can alter the survival rate of a killer more readily than it would one in mid-life.

Young seals or sea lions are preferred over adults, adults rarely being attacked, for adults are dangerous and can cause great injury to the killers. The killers purposely beach themselves upon the land, the pebbled beach, to take a pup in its teeth, pups that consider the shoreline safe and himself out of harm's ways. Killers have mastered this skill which is called 'stranding' and teach it to their young, sometimes in slow motion, and although only a few females participate in securing meals this way all females and juveniles appear to do it, not so much for play, but to harness the skill. Juveniles may strand themselves and adults come to the rescue by stranding themselves alongside, helping them back into the water – some things are not necessarily taught by the mother and it is here that others adults teach the young the skills they need in life to survive. Others may act as decoy, thrashing the water to distract the pups. The killer acts with lightning speed, its dorsal cutting through the water's surface, parallel to the beach and suddenly turns inwards upon the unsuspecting prey. The body is almost entirely out of water when it snatches onto a pup. From here the killer can thrust forward its attack to further beach itself and gain victory if the pup is too far out of reach or simply fall back with their mouth full or empty. It will shake its victim mercilessly in order to disorientate or kill. Killers will take their prey so that the pod can be fed equally, the calves coming first. The claves might even play with the meal, like and adult, harnessing its techniques on the killing of its prey; in its capture, in its demise. Lessons must be learnt and maintained by young and old.

Another method which delivers results is in the case where a seal might hide on the bottom of the sea, in a cave or rock crevice. Two killers will take turns in surfacing and taking a breath, always one maintaining its watch upon the rock crevice, so that once the seal runs out of breath and tries to escape there will be one killer at least to secure the meal.

They can hold their breath for several minutes in a dive of 400 metres or more, where evolution has provided it with unique abilities in its consumption of oxygen. It is able to exchange gasses more readily, each breath being manipulated in different ways to cater for different dives, being shallow or deep. Its rib cage can collapse under pressure from water, surplus air collecting beneath the blowhole in nasal passages, and even more complex to this it is able to store oxygen reserves in its bodily fluid and muscle tissue as well as in the red blood cells. Its heart beat can be slowed, in particular where a deep dive is concerned. Oxygenated blood is also diverted from other muscle and tissue, like the brain and the heart. Most amazingly they can reabsorb, with no effort at all, blood nitrogen, whereby it can avoid the bends which is so common to man, avoiding the formation of nitrogen bubbles in the blood.

Breathing, in particular with respect to smaller groups and a term-based scenario, or where such is deemed appropriate due to depth of dives and the importance of a hunt, can be carried out collectively and for the good of the pod. When many killers are seen to surface at the same time, or within a very short space of time, this is not sheer coincidence but a manipulation which is conducted by all involved in a particular act which deems such to be employed.

When a calf enters its watery world for the first time it gulps in air to satisfy its need to survive, as any living creature will do, and shortly after this the mother and the calf's breathing becomes synchronized and will remain so for much of their lives, their breathing aligned for the benefit of them and the group, the mother becoming somewhat of a conductor of an orchestra whereby the remainder of the pod will take its breathing from her, for the needs of one and all, for the social binding, for the maintenance of life and their constant forage for food.

Generations of hunting tactics are taught to the young, they are shown first-hand how to combine their abilities and this is reflected in their success. Crucial skills are passed down from one generation to the next, both individual and social, all for the securing of food. They acquire the ability to hunt fish on their own at six months and speedily learn vocalizations, echolocation techniques, social protocol and hunting strategies. Calves mimic lessons demonstrated with great patience from mothers and grandmothers.

They usually place great distance between pods and travel in the same direction and when they encounter food they will noisily leap and splash in the water to signify the find or simply send a vocalized message, though use of sonar is questionable due to alerting prey of their presence, in particular dolphins and other mammals.

They devour creatures great and small, fish and whales; whatever they can get their teeth into.

A message is received from another pod, a school of fish close by. Three pods move in and slowly force the school towards the surface. The school is compacted smaller and smaller. They then vocalize their movements in the coordinated attack, flash their white markings to disorientate the herring that immediately panic and set themselves up as a meal. The killers slap the water with their flukes, stunning the herring and take a mouthful or two of their prey. The killers then take turns so that each has an equal share. An orca beneath flashes his white underbelly and the herring continue in their panic, remaining near the surface where they are needed, with no escape and can be easily taking into the mouth. A burst of fluke-bashing is then commanded by the matriarch and the stunned herring are devoured quickly as they float unconsciously. Other orcas continue to keep the herring massed together, corralled and ready for feeding. Another killer gets its fill and retreats, another comes in to feed. Once all have fed and had their fill the killers turn and depart, leaving the remaining herring to disperse into deeper water; bodies that remain afloat, be they full or half devoured, are picked up by birds of prey as they swoop down and take what's left of the pickings.

Others find larger morsels more rewarding. A blue whale, being 18 metres in length is surrounded by a deployed pod. Killers swim either side and below to prevent the whale from making a move towards deep water. They move in closer and at high speed, allowing their presence to be known, maintaining the fear factor, those either side creating white water as they continue alongside the blue whale. Some move to the front to slow the prey, some behind to prevent it turning tail and trying to escape. They disturb the whale's rhythm of breath. They snap their mouths open and closed, gnashing to terrify their prey. The chase continues for 32 kilometres and the blue whale becomes tired. The killers move in one at a time and take great hunks of flesh from the whale, but he swims on. The attack continues for five hours and the killers, either tired or having had their fill, discontinue with the chase, the blue whale continuing on, a great gaping mass of white blubber showing through where it's dorsal once existed, it having being ripped to shreds. Death is just hours away and the blue whale is now a beacon for sharks everywhere, sharks that keep away from the killers, for the killer looks upon the shark as nothing more than a prawn.

Orcas are one of the few animal species to have distinct cultures, and hunting strategies of one orca community are usually unique to that community. Their cultural behaviours are learned behaviours and not instinctive behaviour. When an individual initiates a new behaviour, others will copy and youngsters will be taught by adults. In the case of the seal hunting orcas of Argentina, orcas practice beaching and rescuing themselves and pass the skills on to their offspring in preparation for catching seal pups on the beaches of the seal colonies.

For thousands of years, before man recorded such events, killer whales did hunt all manner of baleen whales in every ocean on this planet, and only once in all that time has it been witnessed, and recorded for the prosperity of understanding and knowledge, that they co-operated with humans in their hunt for whales in one place and one place only. A family which went by the surname Davidson did make a living by the help given in exchange for aid, where the killer whale taxed the human hunt in accordance with their needs: fresh meat, the flesh of the baleen, the unmistakable diet of a particular pod of killers so fondly referred to as friends and co-conspirators, and took place at a place known as Twofold Bay on the east coast of Australia. And it is here that an extraordinary story unfolds of an unwritten contract between man and beast, one of nature's most powerful and intelligent, one that is misunderstood and labelled unkindly. This story of the killer is not meant to specifically qualify anything in particular, nor to superimpose one quality or behaviour over another, yet it is a main jest of this story to reflect upon their character, both man and beast, and the reasons for their co-operation in order for us to grasp a better understanding of the overall picture, and in order to do this we must hear the combined story of both humans and killers alike.

CHAPTER ONE
1862

From a distance the dorsal of the killers can be seen to perforate the surface of the sea, cutting effortlessly through the gentle rolling waves, each of the mammals beneath fully aware of all around them as their flippers help to guide them through the water which encases them.

They surface from time to time, more often than not at around the same time, in particular where a mother and a calf are concerned.

The spouting of water, as air is ejected from the blowhole, looks like that of a great cloud of mist exploding from within; the water dissipates in the air as it gets carried away by the fresh breeze coming up from the south, and they prepare for another dive by sucking in more oxygen.

It is a wonder in itself to see these mushrooming clouds erupt from the killers, unlike the other cloud known by man where devastation rocks the world and kills people in their thousands, an unforseen tragedy which has yet been delivered to the world. There is a calm about it, something surreal, where one can become lost in his dreams, forget his place in the world, sitting back and watching the event unfurl. But an even bigger event is about to take place and far from land, in the tropics and close to Hawaii where the pristine waters are very soon to be visited; but only for a short time.

The matriarch knows of better places in the world, other bays and inlets that she has visited in the past, even for one as young as her.

Her name is Stranger and she is rather young at just 14 years, although she had reached sexual maturity at 11 years of age. She was currently surrounded by members of her pod, other killer whales that had joined her in her adolescence, seeing for themselves that she had great vision and purpose, knew of things that they did not. Stranger had been accepted as their matriarch without argument, setting themselves up beside her so that they could learn to act as one. Even now in the few short years that they had been together their dialect had transposed itself as different from others, a uniqueness unfolding with their traits as a unit. She had fallen pregnant when falling in with a large pod of 'offshore' killers but had soon decided to leave, her mate having decided to remain with his mother and grandmother; for the good of the community as a whole.

There was Typee, and at 23 years of age was the oldest of the pod. He had a mate, a killer whose dorsal was completely bent over; her name was Humpy. Humpy was 17 and she had partnered with Typee several years before, Typee having left his previous pod due to his mother's death. They were of breeding age but had yet shown little reward for their prowess in love-making.

There was also another pair, a male by the name of Cooper and a female by the name of Big Ben. Both were 11 years of age and had coupled many years before, being very dependent on one another and practically inseparable, even when called upon during times of hunting. It was their spirit as a couple, their overwhelming desire to be as one, which had forced them to separate from their larger pod of the Antarctic.

So here they were, a small pod of five that had swollen from one; Stranger was about to give birth and the exploding of their population was just around the corner, for Stranger's abilities in the hunt would become legendary amongst all that they came into contact with, many male and female alike soon to give up their post in their pod to join with hers.

Little communication was shared between the members of the pod as they continued slowly on their way, patrolling the waters far from the main coast, just off Hawaii, communication which is even less used when nearing selected feeding locations, for prey could be almost anywhere, and even though a new mouth was about to be born the killers were always alert for an easy meal.

Searching constantly was their only reward but communication between killers is a natural part of life and so takes place during parts of the day or night that are more appropriate, using dialect which becomes modified over the decades to correspond with a particular pod, regional variations that are perfected and used methodically without thought; it is that which they now suppress.

Being a very social animal, in particular where without a family representative – namely a pod of siblings, brethren, mother and father – they have been know, world-wide, to seek out the company of humans. In this alone we find it hard to believe that creatures of the deep feel as though they have a connection, of any description, with the human race, but they do. They feel the

26

effects of loneliness and embarrassment, as men do, and they experience fear as well, but yet this is far from their minds for a birth is taking place, Tom being delivered·unto the world, and it is now that vocalization can be heard, sound echoes out across the ocean.

The mother's abdomen is swollen with a foetus that has been gestating for 17 months, it's wriggling and squirming within being felt more easily as the days pass Stranger by.

The mother swims around displaying a little discomfort, her restless commotion drawing little concern, and she rises to the surface for breath, remaining there, just below the waves, for the moment is near. She can feel the soft breeze upon her skin, feel the warmth shine down upon her on this marvellous day. Her first born is about to make its way into the world.

She swims about and then suddenly pauses for the birth has commenced. Her flukes and head are lifted up, her back arched; she gives birth whilst amidst the pod, all other killers close by and surrounding her, protecting her in her time of need, watching with baited breath for the first birth of this new pod.

It is normal for the flukes to be seen first, rarely the head, and the calf emerges after just a short period of delivery, contractions having been harnessed in the delivery to reward the mother with a healthy birth. Her thrashing about, which is necessary on some occasions, has provided the reward, the somersaults and barrel rolls aiding a difficult delivery.

The calf is pushed out, Tom jettison delicately away from the mother as Stranger gently accelerates forward (or hastily with much power with a more difficult delivery) and the calf, amidst the red mist of blood from the torn umbilicus, swims immediately (if not clumsily) to the surface just above, to suck in its first breath.

Tom is born; the calf's triangle dorsal fin droops, its fore flippers rigid, and its flukes unfurl and thrashes in the watery world in which it has been born.

Tom is free at last, to swim and splash about, to breathe the air above the surface of the sea.

He is lifted into the air on several occasions and much rubbing of skin on skin takes place for all are overjoyed to see him born unto the world. A little percussive activity now takes place though Tom is not hurt in any way. He will maintain a very close connection with his mother for the first year of his life and even after this, and growing into maturity, will always remain a member of her pod and have close ties with other members too. But for the first year he remains solely in the care of his mother, sheltered by her body, protected by her flippers, provided sanction by the pod.

Stranger is exhausted, but such exhaustion is dependent on the type of delivery, easy or hard. Tom had joined with his mother and both are happy, the ordeal forgotten and far behind them now.

So now they are swimming side by side and commence to breathe in a similar pattern in order to stay close, and the calf out of danger. They have much to be thankful for. But Stranger is a little concerned for there is safety in numbers. More killers in the pod would be welcome however. A matriarch with great hunting ability and strategies to share was worth her weight in gold.

Stranger knew a place not so very far away; a place where hunting whales was a common occurrence. She had seen the pod in action and had even shared in the sport herself. The pod was small but Stranger also knew of another. There were several animals she knew she could influence quite readily.

She would rely on Typee's aid, for he was majestic and quick, good at hunting, good at killing, grand at reading the thoughts of others. He was too much of a commandeering sort to be made the leader of a sub-pod but he had abilities which she could milk. She then reflected upon Typee's mate, Humpy.

Humpy was a vicious type, not afraid to lead a charge, not afraid to take a risk when needed. Stranger would use her as a sub-pod contender when the time was ripe, allow Humpy to remain close by her side. Yes indeed, Stranger would have Humpy as an ally, this would keep Typee close and others even closer, for those intimidated by Typee would be subjected to Stranger's calling.

But there was plenty of time to reflect on tactics, for now she was simply content to see Tom now swimming behind her right flipper, searching for the retractable abdominal nipples and he soon begins to suckle for the very first time. Touch is sensitive and sometimes commanding, where a calf requests feeding from its mother. Nudges, nibbles, and fore-flipper caresses, a bond grows between the two. An orca might even rake its teeth on another's back, cavort and wrestle, but never fight. After some time at feeding, Tom precariously takes up a position behind the dorsal fin to swim effortlessly along in the slipstream created, but soon returns to the protected side for more milk.

Tom is 2.5 metres long and weighs 200kg, a grand specimen.

CHAPTER TWO

In the early Days and beyond, it was well known across the face of the whale fishing industry (apart from the few) that seafaring vessels which frequented the oceans on a regular basis, and for great stints of time, in some cases as long as four years, were more easily controlled by commandeering different nationalities to work upon the ships, and in the case of Australian vessels it was seen that aboriginals and South Sea Islanders were the best breed for manning the vessels, a lesson learnt quickly by the Davidsons and their interactions with the Yuin.

A steep hill reaches for the sky at Snug Cove and here can be seen the town of Eden, upon a saddle in the high ground. It looks down and over the bay, its harbour, where a magnificent blue attracts the eye and sandy beaches of honeycomb break the line between sea and forest surrounds.

The lookout (Boyd's tower on South Head) was severely damaged by lightening in the 1860's and never repaired, but still put to good use; it could be seen for miles out to sea and served whalers well on more than one occasion.

It was back then, in May of 1863, that George Davidson was born in Eden; Alexander's grandson. This was his world now, where the true semblance of a bay whaling station could be seen for what it was, where two weatherboard homes could be seen situated upon the banks near the bay and an open shelter procured from wood sat waiting for whale blubber to be delivered it. Beneath the shelter is the brickwork of the try-works, large iron vats and large tanks for the storing of oil. A windlass would see to it that the carcass was heaved too by way of a large rope, the carcass hauled up and deblubbered. Even when George was crawling upon hand and knees he had become familiar with the boat house where the shelter of 4.6 x 12.2 metres secured the boats employed in the whaling ventures. The boats are shallow and nine metres long, sturdy and ready for rowing, prepared for launch at a moment's notice, only vacant the crew to power them through the turbulence of the sea.

Set upon his way, Alexander Walker Davidson (who was initially Boyd's carpenter), a Presbyterian who believed in treating everyone fairly, including the indigenous crews he hired and paid with a full wage, built a home from the wreck of the Lawrence Frost, along with a boatshed and workshop. The whaling station try-works consisted of iron pots in a shed with a long ramp, and changed little for the entire time that the bay whaling operation remained intact. He had a capstan to haul the quantities of blubber into position for extracting the oil, where 9-inch strips of fat are ripped from the flesh beneath, and when the job is done, all that is left is a carcass of red lying in pools of blood. The Davidson cottages and whaling station was positioned on the Kiah River, across from the town of Eden, on the other side of the bay and away from the mainstream bustle of country life.

31

Many different crews were stationed at Twofold Bay at one time or another, including the Walker Brothers, the Barclays, Rixons, Whelans, Newlands and Powers; but of all the men and boats that were cast into the sea in an effort to kill a whale it was the Davidsons that had secured the majority of assistance offered by the killers, for the killers disliked the explosive harpoons that some crews employed when hunting baleen, modern technology which held little interest for the Davidsons. This favouritism seemed to infuriate the other crews even more, to such a degree that more artillery came into play, which saw to it that the killers assisted the Davidsons only, their green boats easy to identify, not to mention the silhouettes, faces, and characteristics, of those that they had come to know so well; the green colour was in fact based on the traditional Scottish Davidson tartan which was of the same colour.

Davidson and his small band of 5 boats had secured an ally for all time. The Davidsons eventually won the assistance of the killer, all others being ignored by the black and white Wolves of the Sea. This saw great favour shine upon the Davidson's for more than one reason and that is of the decline in the numbers of right whales passing along the coast in tune with the culmination of the hunting of the sperm whale, a decline in numbers which had commenced in Tasmania around 1841.

With learning being a two-way street, and Alexander open to all that the indigenous crews offered, came to understand and put into practise the Law of the Tongue, where for the aid in catching the baleen the killers were permitted to sup on the tongue and lips of all that was caught, not to mention that dorsal fin and body markings were soon recognized as familiar faces and allowed the bay whalers to identify with the individual killers on a name-basis, names which were derived from the Yuin deceased. Particular animals that were given attention over the years were, Tom, Hookey, Humpy, Jackson, Cooper, Charlie, Typee, Stranger, Kinscher, Montague, Old Ben, Young Ben, Sharkey, Jimmy, Brierly, Youngster, Walker, Skinner, Big Jack, and Little Jack, many others remaining anonymous (to the tune of around 50 killers spread over 3 pods, each pod, in some cases, again split into sub-pods) as no records have enlightened us further. It was truly amazing how the killers would cooperate, not just with one another, but also the Davidsons. In a concert of manipulation, and well-tuned and orchestrated manoeuvres, the pods would attend their different tasks like a military juggernaut going through its paces, with one pod positioning itself out to sea to prevent escape and drive in towards the coast, another to cut off any escape to the front of the whales migratory route, and the third to hone in the attack which in some cases could take all day, far less than what could normally be expected if there was no aid to be offered by the skilful throwing of harpoon and lance from the bay whalers upon their little boats. The baleen had no way of escape, even unable to dive, for killers would surround their prey on all sides as well as below, and could even be seen throwing themselves upon the baleen's back in an attempt to smother its blowhole in order to restrict its breathing.

Each year the killer whales moved from their Antarctic station to the coast of East Australia, moving with the weather, following the fresh breeze of winter as it approached the coast and the streamlined move of baleen as they swam to warmer seas. The move into warmer waters during the winter months was not something that could be considered as common amongst other pods, for many remained stationed where food was in its plenty, but the killers of Twofold Bay had learnt to help themselves during hard times. Here they lay, just off the coast, in wait for their prey as they made for the breeding grounds, rarely far from shore, for the migratory routes of the baleen brought the great whales up from the south and along the coastline, past Leatherjacket Bay and then to Twofold Bay. It was at Leatherjacket that the killers initially sprung their ambush in an attack of several phases, one of which was to dispatch one or more of their own towards Twofold Bay where, unbeknown to them, a lookout was positioned at Boyd's tower on South Head, atop the lighthouse that Boyd had abandoned so long ago: not to be confused with the lighthouse above Snug Cove.

The prowling killer, on the loose, searching for his prey; there he was. The sperm whale fed on octopus, the dolphin upon fish, but the black and white of their close relation fed upon them. They fed upon the grampus, seals where available, and whale for their tender choices of lip and tongue. But in most cases the killer whale was after the humpback and lacked much interest in the fin whale and blue for the present, for both were faster in the water, certainly too fast for the rowing power of the men of Eden, unless aided by a pull on the ropes attached to a boat.

This was the pods way of life, the chosen path. Some pods chose to remain in the colder climates, a minority preferred the warmer, but all chose to occupy very large areas and wander with purpose from one region to the next, whether they did so in order to change their diet or not was up to the animals in question. If a particular fish is found to be less unavailable due to its own cycle of life and death then there is good reason for diet change or change of scenery, and preference is always given to survival, in particular the survival of the young.

So it was here that the killers had congregated, seen by few darting eyes from the coast, watching as the identities of those beneath their dorsal glide effortlessly through the water, Tom with his mark and Hookey with his, distinguishing one from the other as the pod makes its way to the grounds which are to become home for the winter months ahead.

Initially the pods are split, one a mile out to sea, another at two miles, and a third at three, set upon an angle in order to channel their pray towards the shore and upheaval, where the crews of Davidson's boats awaited with glee. And then, finally, a cow and her unborn calf make an appearance, heading northward for warmer waters and into the trap.

On seeing the spurts of a whale the lookout would take to his horse and ride at a great pace the six kilometres to the Kiah Inlet only to find that he time had been wasted for, Tom the killer, in more cases than not, had swam to the mouth of the Kiah River, where the Davidsons were housed in two isolated buildings so constructed for life and leisure.

From within the bay, Tom commenced upon alerting the men ashore of the approaching quarry by flop-tailing until such a time that the whalers made their way into the waters of the bay aboard their boats to the waiting escort. The flop-tailing was for the Davidsons alone, and none other, a visitation seen nowhere else in the world. Tom alone, or the small sub-pod of 2-3 killers of which had been detached, would then lead the boats out to where the baleen was growing weary and distressed, more so than to the crews following the glowing bioluminescent trails which would light up the ocean on nights where the moon was not to be seen. It was to become fate, therefore, that Tom would become the most recognisable of all the killers for his regular contact with them saw to it that their trusting relationship did grow, regardless of his sometimes annoying and playful nature.

The harpoon is thrown and sticks fast. HOORAH! bellows out for all to hear, for the whale has been stuck well, the unborn calf moving inside her, the mother's fear for her young making itself present upon the minds of the killers, and the killers like what they register and feel, for the fear within the humpback will be her own undoing. STERN ALL! then becomes clear and the boat is dragged, all oars pulled in unison with great strength, pulled back in order to aid in the slowing of the leviathan, and escape from threat as the whale turns abruptly and the water surges in greats masses, the boat bobbing about upon the waves of the sea and the turbulence of the fight. The boat was built for the stresses of the fight, pointed at both ends for easy momentum forward and aft, made of good cedar and built to last, but nothing could handle the thrashing flukes of a whale gone mad.

In the unforseen misfortune of a capsized boat the killers would also assist with the charged duty of ensuring their safety by swimming around the boat's crew and protecting them from the sharks drawn haphazardly to the commotion of the fight against the whale and the men's struggle to stay afloat in rough seas. Tom was truly a member of the family and trusted heavily. Such damage to boats was seen often, caused by the baleen in their effort to survive, and it was here that the Davidsons did well, for the maintenance of the boats and equipment was kept in-house, Alexander's son, John, helping with carpentry skills that put most to shame, and aid was also sought in regards to manning boats in the form of the Davidson cousins, the Greig family.

CHAPTER THREE

George Davidson in 1877, now 14 years old, was soon to commence upon his own whaling journey through the decades by picking up the struggle against the sea at the same time that sperm whaling was considered by many as a thing of the past, for the drain upon their schools – or pods – had proven fatal for the industry which saw them slaughtered to near extinction. He wasn't tall in stature but was to become respected amongst his peers and others far away, to be placed within the annals of history, to be toasted as a most remarkable man. But now, as a boy turning into a man, his strengths were both hard and easy to see and all he could do was dream of what was soon to be a reality.

He had a spring in his step, walked with arms swinging as though without a care in the world, confident but certainly never cocky or juvenile. He bore a distinctive arch upon his nose and his eyes were a clear blue; most remarkable and hypnotising, though in a friendly way. He wished to be a whaler, like his father, and his wish was about to become true.

He stood upon a hill and watched as the men battled against a leviathan of the sea, gaining ground on the whale; it would be his turn soon. George was utterly astounded, to a great degree, on how the killers felt the prolonged urge, or requirement, or need, to lay visit upon Twofold Bay, every year, one after the next, not missing a single season; but still, they returned, like a gathering of children to their place of birth. Even with the exceptional hearing of the whales within their environment it did come to pass that the occasional humpback was missed by the pod of killers; but it wasn't so much as missed but more to the point that the pod was making a decision on the best form of attack and which whale to take down first. Scenarios had to be measured and food secured, so the pod would always make a preference in favour of themselves. But from the crew's point of perspective the situation was more widely varied and it was the humans who had failed to see a particular whale and not the other way around. The Davidson's would hit the surface of the water to alert the whales to the presence of a humpback and their current position, the killers turning in unison to accept the ultimatum, for it would save them much time in bringing down a whale with the help of the harpoon and lance, regardless of their strategic position.

Tom could see, feel and hear the other killers around him, those of the pod in which he belonged, the pod belonging to Humpy.

Humpy commanded over the pod with extreme precision, courtesy and steadfast will, leading by example and displaying a great understanding of those within her pod and of those that were about to be eaten, but before the formalities of the hunt could take place they were to be joined once more with the matriarch (Stranger) and the others.

A ceremony was about to take place, one that occurred from time to time when one of the pods of related killers joined back together after a degree of absence, having gone their separate ways in forage and exploration. The two pods were lined abreast, opposite each other, facing one another once more and preparing to be joined again as one. Slowly but surely both groups approached one another, drawing closer, closer the gap. They were now at 20 metres apart and they came to a stop, sounding delicately their calls, looking upon one another over the space between them. Then, after half a minute of ceremonial action the two groups swam towards each other and submerged, to surface shortly after, mingles again as one entity, a single pod. They were now ready for the hunt, changing their diet to match their tactics, for the lead up to this day saw the killers in their smaller group's source other prey of smaller girth.

Now the pods of strengthened unity move towards Twofold Bay for they have heard the movement of a whale close by and they soon find themselves in the fight for food.

The baleen puts up a grand resistance, stubborn and worthy to be called a whale.

From time to time the killers of the pod would vacant themselves from their watery surrounds and propel themselves upon the back of the whale, to cover its blowhole and prevent it from breathing, aiding the efforts to drown the beast so that a meal could be secured. The whale would usually try to then sound (dive) but its efforts to do so would be warded off by killers beneath.

Another animal suddenly shoots itself out of the water in order to block the blowhole, a gasp for air in the build-up of fear denied the pregnant humpback. It is as though the whale is under protective custody, flanked by killers. Others further out to sea now act upon the calls, some heading to the front of the chase to slow the escape down and others to help with the capture, a concerted effort by all, and none will go without a meal, the youngest being fed first, regardless of their actions within the act of the kill.

The stress within the humpback mounts quickly but doesn't peak; it just keeps on growing, the whale's thoughts falling upon the unborn calf that she carries, the calf that she has been carrying for eleven months and two weeks – on the verge of giving birth. It is so obvious, even to this humpback of little experience, that there will be no solace from the predicament she is in. She had departed the waters of the Antarctic some time ago, to make way for the traditional breeding grounds further north, following the coastline as close as she dared for she was alone and without company; as this is the way that most travelled.

The humpback's concern now was for the safety of her unborn, and although she soon realised that she would no longer voice her songlike choruses to the world around her, or even behold the loving sweetness of weaning her young over the next eleven to twelve months, she had to try.

A killer made another strike upon her frail body of twelve metres, one that had been supporting her and the unborn, another chunk of blubber being taken from her flank, the pain searing via shooting pains through her body, triggering receptacles within her, further thrashing of her body hence erupting from within.

What had she done to deserve such torment before death and was her unborn still alive or dead? She shook the thought from her mind, to seek the only option open... complete and utter survival. She wished to feed again upon the capelin, herring, mackerel, and sand lance, to feel the wonder of feeding, to swim open mouth, water goes in and out through side plates leaving the food behind, or to simply open her mouth, take in as much water as possible, and then close her mouth once more, forcing the water out through plates leaving the meal behind: it was all much the same. If she didn't fight now then there would be no tomorrow, never again would she feel the thrashing of fish against her 380 baleen plates, the comb-like plates covered in a series of olive-black bristles, never again to feel the warmth of a full stomach. But now... now she could see death on the horizon but fought on heroically, the fight for survival taking control over her every movement.

And it is now that the bay whalers make their first appearance, to aid in the killing of the whale, to help provide sustenance to the pods, and they don't disappoint, being very quick with decision and action, even if late and after much effort and energy on behalf of the killers has been depleted.

The harpooner exchanges places with the headsman as quickly as possible, the headsman positioning himself and readying a lance for the killing to begin, the lengthy hours that lay ahead, the cold of the night to be endured, the thirst, the rapture, the torn muscle and sore throats. And with the concerted efforts of gigantic proportion the killing of a whale could take quite some time but the strain of the fight being more equally shared between human and orca.

Tom would quite often be seen to jostle with the rope fastened to a harpoon, enjoying himself more than ever, hanging onto the harpoon line for anything up to 30 minutes, being dragged along by the force of the humpback as it made its way through the surging sea walls which grew and then subsided, being dragged along like a dead weight, the surges of white water turning over upon the surface of the sea; he did this by biting upon the rope and holding it in his mouth or simply placing it beneath one of his flippers. Tom was not a mature animal, to say the least, but his efforts in the catch would still be rewarded with an equal share of lips and tongue.

The battle continues well into the night, lances thrown with great effort, to be placed between the ribs of the whale being targeted, to penetrate deep and cause that very inflicting and deadly wound; and the incorrect placement of a lance would see the effort wasted, for little damage may be done, or the lance might simply fall out and sink to the floor of the sea, equipment lost forever, never to be retrieved. The moon then shows itself and then, with sudden realisation, the men stand up and cheer aloud for blood comes rushing from the blowhole of the humpback, the best sign ever to indicate that the kill is almost secured, and with the rushing of red into the air around them the whale commences with its death flurry, the piercing red pain of one or more wounds growing in torment. The end is so very near and the humpback knows without a doubt that she will never get to share the next two years of bonding with her unborn. And then the end is met.

The joy of the win is exuberating to say the least, man and beast receiving great joy from what they have achieved, their combined effort rewarding both parties.

The men commence about the task of attaching an anchor to the carcass as fresh as it is, the killer whales moving in for their prize. The killers force open the humpback's mouth as the men continue their work, forcing their way into where the tongue sits ready, ready to be devoured. Calves are fed first and then all those that remain take turns, none taking more than they should; all is shared equally. By the time the first of the killers have fed the others have moved in from far out to sea, where the flanks were protected, preventing escape, for the humpback had to be kept as close to shore as possible – inside the bay itself would have been most welcome.

The tongue is completely gone, eaten away, nothing left remaining, and the lips are munched on, ripped apart, taking into the killers' jaws. It is also around this time that the anchor has been well secured and the crew has turned to make headway for home, to return the following day to claim the carcass, when the gases of putrefaction has seen to it that the body resurfaces, usually in 24 hours; sometimes sooner, sometimes a little later.

The killers continue with their feeding, taking the last of the lips into their mouths, finishing up with the last of what they wish and now undertake the last act of their silent agreement. The killers grab the humpback's head, flukes and flippers, and take it down into the depths, to be left near the ocean floor, away from the worst of the swelling sea and turbulence, for it to rest in peace before it is time to be exhumed.

Yeah; that's what George saw, without a mistake, looking out over the bay, having watched the scene unfold and end the way it had; it was breathtaking, and many more days similar to this one were to unfold before his very eyes, before he himself made ready upon the boat and became a whaler.

CHAPTER FOUR

Two boats spearheaded towards the open sea, heading towards the entrance of the bay, both boats competing for the prize that they had to have, for without the oil from the whale their children would go hungry; but the years did not favour too many partnerships competing for the same whale, and competition within Twofold Bay soon subsided over time until there were just a few other hindrances in the way of the Davidson's vision to be the only whalers in the bay.

Each boat surged forward, shoulders rolling, oars in hands, and five oars apiece; but the harpooner of Davidson's crew was already contemplating the desertion of his position, to take his post with his thigh placed in the concave of his thwart, to ready with a harpoon. The, most sudden-like, there was a great spout of water erupting from the surface of the bay, where a right whale had surfaced most temporarily, the water foaming for an instant and the being disrupted by the gigantic lifting of the flukes, the ever dangerous tail then quickly disappearing back into the sea, diving once more after having replenished its breath. A split second later and the unmistakable dorsal of Tom erupted from the water as his entire body lifted out and seemed to freeze, for just a second, in mid-air; it was like a holy man witnessing a true vision of the Mother Mary.

Jackson was alongside Tom and now headed to his port side, endeavouring to cut off the right whale's dive, but little good it would do either, for the harbour was restriction enough, but Jackson was also aware of a possible retreat gained from beneath the waves, where the harpoon and lances of those upon the boat could not see or reach.

George could be seen, his silhouette upon a hill, overlooking the cliff where he stood, watching as the two crews sweated it out, thrashing at the sea with all their strength, trying with all their power to be the first within distance of the whale, to hurtle a harpoon against the great mass that had temporarily disappeared from view. It was George's dad, John Davidson, his jet-black beard upon his face. It was his boat against another, a boat manned by Bob Love, the competition between each extremely fierce, as could be told by the screwed up looks upon their faces, and where every muscle tore at the oars. This was the fight of champions, where the rule of the 'fast fish' is what mattered the most.

The sea was choppy and breeze non-restricting, the freshness doing little to upset the situation, but the work was hard enough. And as the oars continued to beat at the sea from within the security of the row-locks, the Davidson crew stroked ahead, making more ground than Love, making that extra asserted effort to make the grade.

John looked behind him to realise the headway they had gained on the opposition, seeing the sun as it commenced to set behind the bulk of Mount Imlay, a second of mesmerised freedom settling upon his soul, for this was his home, where waves of gentle surf plunged upon the rocks at the foot of the cliffs, where the swells of undulating sea moved within the bay as though caressing the earth beneath, and then towards the mouth of the Kiah River, where long waves of white water broke along Whale Spit, an elongated portion of beach that sheltered, to some degree, the river beyond. Some debris from the 'Lawrence Frost' could still be seen sticking out of the spit, from which the two cottages above were made, buildings painted in white and used for the enterprise of whaling.

The fight beneath the waves continued, the killers trying with all their effort to prevent the right whale from getting past them and on out to sea, but even if such a move was possible and the manoeuvre successful, the whale would still have to contend with the other pod further out, those awaiting the call to join in on the feeding of lip and tongue. Their patience was their virtue.

Tom then abandoned his manoeuvre and raced to the surface, for the whale was changing direction as surely as they had thought, and whilst the other killers, both Jackson and Humpy made the effort to impede on the right whale's progress, Tom broke the surface and half turned, crashing down upon his flank and turning to face the crew of the green boat. He looked upon them momentarily, trying to gain their attention, and John, the headsman, saw what was to play before his very eyes. He had seen Tom do this before but could not clarify what it was that was passing between them both. Tom seemed to look at him directly in the eyes, communicating his dire need.

Tom then turned into the choppy waves and sped off, leading the boat to where the whale was to surface when next requiring a breath of air. Tom was showing them the way, and John saw all the cards fall into place, the connection between Tom's antics of the past and the commotion being performed before him this minute. They were being escorted from the front, shown the way as any usher would do, and Tom wished nothing more than to assist as best he could in the demise of the right whale.

The dark flesh of Sam stood out, easily seen by Tom. He knew then that the harpoon would fly soon enough. Sam placed the end of his oar into a socket opposite the thole-pins. The harpoon was then picked up and position sought. He barely had time to place the weapon upon his right shoulder, a grasp taken upon the shaft of iron, when Tom veered to the right and the whale surfaced briefly between the killer and the crew, but it was brief enough.

Sam hurtled the harpoon forward and down, into the fatty layer and penetrating deep beneath the dorsal. The whale lunged forward with a suddenness expected, water splashing over the crew as they pulled back on the oars, the manila secure to the harpoon, the line tight but able to run freely through the loggerhead if required. All oars were now quickly peaked, pulled from the water in hurried unison, secured into position and out of harm's way, well clear of the surface of the sea which could snap an oar instantly or see to it that one was delivered with great wretchedness against the body of flesh and bone of the man that held it, crippling a crew member beyond expectation.

The right whale thrashed mightily and dived, the boat surging forward under great duress, John manipulating the sweep in a manner of grasp and control that was hard to match, watching the right whale and the surge of the sea as carefully as one could, considering all possibilities, watching for that dreaded moment when the whale might quite easily turn tail and surface from beneath the boat, or simply capsize it by turning swiftly and with great thundering power.

Tom looked back again, seeing the harpoon stuck fast and considered for a brief moment the other crew, Bob Love and his effort to stay put, continuing on in the hope that the harpoon might break clear of the right whale or that another might surface for him to call his own.

John now stood as Sam drew closer, the two exchanging posts, Sam taking up the sweep and John moving to the front of the boat, to prepare the lances for action, to get ready with the actual killing of the whale.

Tom now acted accordingly and dove beneath the surface where Humpy and Jackson continued to harass the right whale, prevented him from diving and heading out to sea. He then turned and headed to the surface, surging out of the water and upon the whale's back, trying with all his might to cover the blowhole of the right whale, to prevent it from breathing properly, to hurry up the arrival of death.

The first lance was then thrown, it penetrating deep and between the ribs, exactly where it was aimed, and the right whale began moving around in circles, taking the boat and its crew with him, John throwing another lance which also hit its mark and within minutes a spout of red erupted from the blowhole after an extraordinarily short dive.

The whale was dead but the deal not completed. John saw, as the others did, that Tom and the others were moving in on the 14 metre long carcass. With quickness delivered they set about tying an anchor to the right whale and a buoy, too, and then set it adrift, to sink to the ocean floor, where the killers could have their feed and the gasses would form within the whales gut, to float again in a days' time, to be collected and drawn into the try works for deblubbering after the killers had fed upon the lips and the tongue.

The call was made and the pod out to sea came thundering in, another to the north of the migratory route also making for the site of the kill, where each and every one of them would get their just reward, none more than another, all equally shared between them, for there was more to come in the following days and weeks, with or without the help of the Davidson's, though help was a benefit to the killers for their energy reserves would not be depleted.

Stranger watched with anticipation over the feeding, ensuring that none of those under her sway took more than their fair share, but greed wasn't something strived for in killer whales, wasn't even a contemplation of mind. These mammals were one and the same, of the same pod, of the same line. They owed one another more than any man could realise, for each one acted in accordance with the will of the others. Sure, they were individuals, each could think for his or her self, but their pod was their religion; was their faith; was everything to them.

Humpy was looked upon as a strong leader, and Stranger knew her well, but she also looked to her young, both Tom and Hooky.

Hooky was a male, as per Tom, and only four years younger; again born of a father that she would never see again. Stranger, matriarch of all before her preferred it this way, preferred to partner with fathers of her off-spring that would have little sway in the years that fell behind them, for Twofold Bay was unique to her and all those that followed.

And so; Typee, Humpy, Cooper, Big Ben, Tom, Hooky and Jackson, all favourites of their matriarch, all known to the men aboard the green boats, had their way with the whale before swimming off towards Leatherjacket Bay for some hard-earned rest, and the other 30 members of their small community followed.

CHAPTER FIVE

George's task at the beginning of his long and rewarding career – rewarded by the love of what he did, not the monetary reward – was to assist his Uncle Jim upon the lookout of square shape and footing, which had be leased by his father... in fact, all the land from South Head to the Kiah River had been leased by him, and this gave him the desired advantages over his competitors. Not only did he have the best post for which to look for whale sign, but also the killers to help with the catch of a prized casket of oil.

Boyd's Tower was still a very fitting building, even with the damage of the storm so many years before, and the visual graces of the sea from South to North was an ally of strategic importance for it meant that the Davidson crews could be launched before all others, and in the case where whale sign was missed, there was the comfort in knowing that Tom would be flop-tailing to his heart's content, drawing their attention to the fact that whale was coming. Jim quite often found himself straddled upon his horse, racing towards the Kiah, raising the alarm of an approaching whale, the sound of the hooves, in particular in the still of night, providing further advance of the news to come, news which was acted upon immediately, even before Uncle Jim had the opportunity to unhorse himself.

On this particular morning, George was to accompany his father in the boats, all three being launched and making their way across the smooth surface which reflected the clear skies high above, moving out towards the mouth of the bay in order to commence with their morning patrol, to search for whale sign, to hope that their efforts would be rewarded by a quick catch and an early lunch – which rarely ever eventuated.

They worked the oars hard and moved out towards the shelter at South Head where a large rock, the colour of red, acted as a wharf, where, very close by a cave of substantial size which provided them with adequate cover from inclement weather. Stores for the cave and the lookout were displaced and the crews on the move once more, making the most of the opportunity to be in the right place and at the right time.

As they stroked the sea and moved out of the heads they could see the spouts of several killers nearer to Leatherjacket Bay. They seemed relaxed and complacent, neither thrashing about, flop-tailing, nor making a general nuisance of themselves as was so common with Tom. Further behind there was another, the waterspout jettison from within its hide whilst surfacing was in progress, the force pushing with it much water, the warmth of the killers interior providing sufficient temperature that when the blow came it was with much mist, the water condensed to form a cloud of spray that mystified any experiencing the sight for the first time.

They were at work, listening intently on the movement of the sea, trying to catch that ever elusive signal that a whale might be approaching or moving a little further out to sea. And that was the real concern. The pods were positioned in good fashion, three pods of equal strength at different intervals from the coast, to act as a curtain for any approaching prey, but if a whale was to be moving further out than expected the killers would have to make their move and try with all their effort to force their prey in towards the killing ground where the men would be ready with harpoons and lances; although in all reality the effort and wasted energy did not always give good cause for a chase to be undertaken and the lessons of years past proved that a whale would be alone... sooner or later.

Tom saw the patrol of three boats and summed up the action, realising that the men were doing as he was doing, patrolling the ground and waiting for their opportunity to strike, in unison if possible. He now turned around and moved stealthily towards the others of his pod, each conserving their energy for when the need arose, waiting patiently and with a skill that had been perfectly engineered over centuries of evolution. It was then that a signal was received from several miles out to sea, that a small whale was bypassing the mouth of Twofold Bay, a minke whale with unborn calf, a small whale which the killers favoured over others but for the moment didn't really provide sufficiently for three pods of gnarled teeth. The killers' jaws opened and closed several times in quick succession, noisily clapping the jaws together in mounting aggression and to press the fear of the impending doom to come deep within the minke's mind. With their mouths closed tight they now shifted into higher gear, the teeth of the upper jaw fit snugly into the gaps provided by the teeth of the lower, so the fitting of one into the other resembled the cogs of a wheel.

The signal was their call to duty and unbeknown to the men in the boats the killers took off beneath the surface of the sea to begin the chase, to pester and provoke, to bring the whale down by all means possible so that sustenance could be gained. The minke would be fairly easy to catch but not really worth the small effort for it would do little in helping hold back the tide of hunger in all the hungry mouths looking forward to a good meal. But the facts of the case were mounted as normal and no single food source shrugged off as dreary. He would provide a little sustenance and wouldn't tax them too much, and hopefully there might be more than one, but regardless of the situation which was currently unavailable to Tom and the pod, the minke was now fully aware of the killers presence, for the signal had been sent, the alarm bells ringing, and the getaway had commenced.

The normal procedure for a the killers of Eden to undertake when hunting a minke was to see it stranded in the shallows and then consumed of all it had to offer, and although the same size as the killers, was certainly unable to outrun it and was entirely out of its class when being run down; in particular where a large pack of hungry mouths were looking for a quick fix.

The minke swam through the sea, the beak and pointed shape of his head gliding through the water, nine metres in length and powering along at great speed, but not fast enough. Her body was streamlined, fins pointed at the tips, and flukes broad and concave along the notched rear margin. It dove then, arching the tail stock high but the flukes remained beneath the waves, the commencement of a deep dive being commenced. The effort was keenly cut off by two killers and the minke was forced to surface, surrendering itself to further torment as mouths tore great chunks out of her flank, all eager to kill her. The rush of red billowed out and merged with the sea, a large cloud expanding out, growing bigger and bigger. Several sharks in the vicinity could hear the calling, the dinner bell ringing, but fear stopped them from approaching too close, for even the great white shark feared the hungry and gluttonous killer, be it one or a hundred.

The three pods gave chase and made ground upon the minke in remarkably quick fashion and soon had her surrounded, the bulge in her undeniable, easily seen for what it was. The unborn calf would also provide great nourishment for the killers who in their ultimate wisdom would take more than the lips and tongue, for although the minke wasn't scrawny, it was simply not enough. Each knew without doubt that the preference would be for a larger baleen to tempt their desire but the minke was not something that went by the way. Many of those in the pods at the present quite preferred the flesh of smaller whales and dolphins, porpoises and fish, but reward was an uncanny infection, in particular where men from boats would freely assist in their downfall.

The minke was a krill feeder, harmless and often alone and today she was to see her end, the end of her life and the unborn calf, the one in her womb that she had not yet got to know and would often treasure the thoughts of future commitments to come.

Tom got to the site of the killing at the same time that the others had had their way with the minke, enough left to feed on but the delicacy gone and forgotten. Share for the sake of sharing, for the needs of the group, for the desire to remain in community spirit and be unselfish as always; but first in, best dish; the unwritten law that ferried from pod to pod, a rehearsed consequence of life which transpired over all else.

Tom tore at what little remained along with the others of his flock, those of his pod that had been the furthest from the find and patrolling their ground as good killers should. The situation was shrugged off and normal patrol duty assumed immediately, the pods returning to their station post haste, silence once again restored and the tranquillity of the sea took hold.

CHAPTER SIX

A great anxiousness fell over them all, heart throbs pushing the excitement of the word to the culmination for their wits end, and the it came again; RUSHO!

George burst through the door and exclaimed through sheer exhilarated enthusiasm for the crew to man the boats, for a whale had been seen, and no sooner were hands on boats then Tom could be seen flop-tailing to the front the Kiah River Bar where the calm surface of the bay splashed pleasurably upon its sands. Even now, as men threw themselves upon the thwarts, grabbing at their oars and thrusting them into the water via the thole pins, jackets were pushed aside and boots forced on by the few that hadn't time to respond to the words that flew through the air of this bright day, the afternoon air fresh with several clouds racing across the sky.

All indications were that it could become a long night affair if the sun was to fall from view. A quick kill was required; if the whale was not secured by nightfall the air would become as uncomfortable as a hindered sea on any stormy day, for wind-chill was always a factor.

Tom, having seen the rush of men to boats, assured of their fast action and soon-to-be presence, turned tail, his flukes thrashing at the surface as he sounded for a little depth, picking up immediately on the situation with the right whale, sending signals through the water.

Tom was no different than any other killer and had normal hearing as well as echolocation. Orcas possessed the ability to see, with quite remarkable vision, both above and below the surface of the sea. Aerial scanning was referred to as 'spy hops' and was where killer whales lifted their heads out of the water to see, but where light quickly dissipates in respect to depth the killer had no alternative but to employ another means of hearing and sight.

Tom was some distance from the fight at the present and could hear without much trouble the thrashing flippers, flukes, and bodies in the water, but a clearer picture of the scene was an advantage to Tom as he sped off wearily towards the right whale.

Echolocation engulfed the area, penetrating all that was literally aimed for, the picture being painted in strong transcendent colours, echolocation being the sensitive sensory system based on sound. It was ten times more accurate than the best sonar in submarines, echoes generated by short pulses of sound directed out to sea to their front. Pulses were emitted via staccato styles, high-frequency sounds that lasted but for a few milliseconds, produced in the nasal passage and deeper, below the blow hole, directed to his front, passing through fatty tissue which acted as a lens (known as 'melon' – its bulging forehead).

He continued focussing the sound in the direction that the killer required as he swam effortlessly through the water. Many segments of the emitted sounds were refracted back, the segments painting the picture as sound returning through thin bony walls of

Tom's lower jaw and transmitted along the jaws length to acoustic conduits before reaching the sensory organs of the middle ear on either side of the skull near the base of the brain. This was an ultrasound in effect where a clear picture of what rests ahead could be formed and acted upon instantly. The returning sound, travelling at four times greater speed than that through the air, provided detailed information on texture, size, shape, distance, and composition.

Tom zoomed in then on the object and bombarded it with further scrutiny, gathering further information, much more precise than before, and above the surface the race continued unabated.

As immediately as they met the first of the waves then the heat of the work commenced to mount, a blanket of false-security against what could well be a night of mounting displeasure.

Three boats mused to pull in unison at first, in file, though slightly askew, each beckoned by their headsman to be the first in range for a harpoon to be thrown, colourful language filling the air, being carried haphazardly across the bay and to the few that watched from the banks, those watching from afar taking little heed as to the words of encouragement as though water off a duck's back, for the language was a part of bay whaling as was lancing or deblubbering. And the voiced encouragement continued and the erupted into a symphony of chorused bellows, for one of their competitors could be seen launching two boats, oars striking the water with as much unrestrained and unchecked jubilance as John Davidson's crews had performed.

Spray lifted from the bows as muscles taunt and pressed for a little extra speed, surmounting efforts of gigantean proportion being reflected on all faces as teeth were exposed to the world and grimaces painted deep lines of passive aggression upon their faces.

This was a race for survival, for the promise of wages, for the security of their families. Each and every one that manned an oar put in an effort that dwarfed all else and the headsmen's efforts at the stern pertained no less, each one full of character and measured agility, controlling their sweeps and looking forward, providing direction and instilling confidence, encouragement and threats of sackings if they were not the first to net the 'fast fish'.

The pod of killers today only numbered three, others stationed further out for there was another whale which had bypassed their trap. Nevertheless the tactics of the day for the pod of three didn't vary from their normal procedures.

Tom returned to reform the threesome, acting upon their instincts and harrying throws, wrestling with great torment the right whale as it was slowly turned towards the mouth of the bay and towards the boats that drew closer and closer with every passing second, oars thrashing at the surface of the sea, boats surging forward towards their victory or demise.

The killers had turned the right whale and it commenced to head for the boats, strung out as they were. The gap between the three warring parties now closed at a tremendous rate and the right whale sounded one more time, disappearing most temporarily from the surface for one of the three killers positioned itself haphazardly beneath the leviathan, preventing it from diving deeper, restricting its movement as though by leash, forcing it to surface before its time.

The disruption in the contour of the bay's surface drew the immediate attention of those in Whelan's front contender, the uplift of water created by the whale as it surfaced bringing a little more than surprise to dawn upon their faces, and as the back of the whale broke the seal between water and air the bow of

Whelan's boat was lifted with no effort whatsoever upon the crest of their passion's bulk.

Oars were lifted out of the water, still in their thole pins, riding high for the briefest of seconds, and not milliseconds before men began to consider jumping from the peril of an unstable and contemptuous predicament the boat slid harmlessly back into the chop of the waves and the oars were once again handled accordingly.

Tom took an instinctive second to peruse the situation above, lifting his eyes out of the water to look up the position of the crew's and their boats of glorious empowerment. A green boat was close to Whelan's, so close in fact that the harpooner stood ready, weapon of trade upon his shoulder, thigh braced against the thwart and ready to fling with great accuracy his iron. It left his hand and fell towards the right whale but there was insufficient power behind the throw, a somewhat underestimate of Pigeon, the last throw he would ever make, for the loss of the whale meant his immediate termination from employment, sufficient evidence being accumulated over the past weeks to indicate that Pigeon had been paid-off by Whelan himself.

But the task at hand was still afloat, harried continuously by the killers, and as the jaw of John Davidson dropped in disbelief the man of Whelan's second boat, known by all as Bedford, tossed his harpoon with great victory, a mass of energy, precision, and testimony to his ability, securing itself hard.

The 'fast fish' had been achieved by Whelan and the lancing began, Davidson's boats moving aside and waiting to see if the harpoon were to fall from grace, but it was not to eventuate.

There was no escaping the trap, even with the gigantean effort of the right whale as it sprang for the mouth of the bay and the wide-open sea, pulling the boat in tow, attached quite securely by harpoon and manila rope, never to abscond from its delivery upon the ramps of the try-works with the windlass working to its fullest potential.

John saw the dilemma as it was and fell upon the only conclusion; the battle had been lost due to the unfettered conviction of one of his own men, a soon-to-be figure on the unemployment line or working for his opposition, but the opposition would not last, for the end was being delivered to them this very minute.

Davidson and his three crews could not believe their eyes as the whale gave up its fight for life, sooner than expected and pelted well by the two boats that were positioned one on either side. If it hadn't been for the help provided by the killers, then the kill would have been enduring to say the least. And now, in the cold victory that had been won, Whelan was towing the carcass in towards his workshop, to be deblubbered then and there, towed under the power of two boats, delivery assured. And as the boats tugged on their oars the three killers came in for their reward, trying with great effort to get close enough for them to sup on the lips and the tongue.

Some of Whelan's men picked up a tool-of-the-trade that had been stowed aboard, razor-sharp boat spades, square in shape and very sharp, normally used for deblubbering. They were striking at the killers, keeping them at bay, holding back their attempts to take their reward, denying them their means to survive.

Tom surfaced and looked the men in the eyes, one at a time and summed them up. He took note of the boats and remembered them well. Davidson's boats were green and never shied from providing the reward for their combined victory over a whale, but these others... who were they? What were they playing at? They would be remembered and never forgotten, and never again would another be given the opportunities of the hunt which only the killers could provide... unequivocal assistance... never again would another boat be provided as much as a wink of recognition or assistance.

CHAPTER SEVEN

The sun had not even commenced to light the day when two of the killers commenced flop-tailing in front of the Kiah Inlet, throwing themselves out of the sea to crash upon the rolling waves, the wind strong and cold but not as bad as some mornings the men had come to know.

Weather was an important factor in the industry, in particular where the crews were concerned. A hard south-west wind was cold and its after-affect was that it brought the sea up: choppy in the bay and out by the mouth of Twofold Bay, and further out the swells and disturbance upon the sea would be in full effect. Factors: a mind full of what-ifs. The ground swell may take place and yet again the wind could change direction as opposed to dropping off and push the bad weather closer into shore. But at present all was fine.

RUSHO!

And the chase was on.

George was fourteen, full of vigour and extremely keen: 1877.

Arms found their way into jackets as the figures, dark upon the backdrop of the ground around them, running as fast as they could towards the boats, dashing out of the bunkhouse like greyhounds on the loose and after a hare. The night revealed further information, enlightenment as to the source of the killers means to attract the bay whalers, for the unmistakable sound of a humpback could be heard in the distance, somewhere just inside the mouth of the bay, where many more killers were present and attempting with all their might to keep the whale from heading out to sea, trying to force it further into the bay where it would be stuck between a rock and a hard place, between killers of sea and land, where mammals of flippers and men's hands could come together and contemplate great celebration on the killing of another humpback. The killers could taste the tongue and they moved into position, and the headsman was considering the tonnage of oil that might be obtained from the fish in the bay.

The men wasted no time at all in closing the gap between themselves and the fray, battling the resistance offered by the sea as they powered along, muscles burning at the effort which each man poured into the task. And the dark of the night was temporarily forgotten as they pushed on towards the noise in the distance, knowing full well that the killers had a large humper to contend with.

The light of the bunkhouse and the cottage now far behind them gradually grew smaller and smaller. There was no light of the moon to aid them but it was a cloudy night above and reflections from the sun shining bright upon the crust of the earth, from somewhere far over the horizon, shed little light upon their world, the stars above adding nothing of worth, but all bay whalers know of one thing that could be counted on when stalking a whale at night, in particular where the killers were concerned, and that was the clear presence of the phosphorescent trails that cut tracks upon the sea, a navigational aid which paved the way to where the whale was waiting, killers harrying as they did so well.

George sat upon in front of the forward most thwart and did what he could with providing direction, though the headsman, his father, needed little prompting as the trails left by the killers were easy to follow. Two of the great whales then moved back to see what was wrong with the boat, to see if there was something amiss, for the killers felt as though the men in their tubs were not performing their tasks in an adequate fashion.

Tom pushed against the lead boat, shoving it sideways, endeavouring to point out that he could aid the boat if only they were to think on the situation. If a harpoon had been thrown then there would be a rope, a rope which could be pulled by Tom to aid the boat in gaining speed and much time. With the absence of the rope there was little Tom could do and wrestling with the progress of the boat was doing little to invoke the imagination of those rowing.

Tom took off then, a few curses from the men aboard rising into the air, voices that bellowed out for miles and miles, to die upon the wind which commenced to grow its ferocity, the cold night air now stinging at the men's faces for the spray of the ocean, coming up from the rolling waves and the bow of the boat, commenced to make itself known to the rowers, each and every one feeling the chill commence to grow, even in the heat of the moment where muscles stun at the work they performed.

The headsman ordered for silence for the last thing he wished was for any competitor to hear them chasing down another whale. They had lost one just the day before and another would just not do. They were heading towards Middle Head now, past Snug

Cove and Eden, where the sleeping town winked once or twice, a lantern being lit from there upon the shore.

Tom and two others were moving just below the surface, the bulges of sea moving with them, the tops of their backs and a little of their flukes seen from time to time due to the most temporary appearance of the moon. They were pestering the whale to no avail.

The night was dark and spy-hopping was no guarantee of good visual contact with either the men on the boats or with the whale as it surfaced, blowing out and breathing in more air. The killers decided on another action, to force the whale deeper, to see it use its air once and for all, to deplete it emphatically of its facility and drown it then and there. This was the thought that ran through the killers, the tactic they would employ, and deprive the men above of the ability to anchor the carcass. If the weather failed to improve, and got any worse, the carcass could well drift out to sea before they had the opportunity to bring it ashore. But Tom knew as well as the others that they needed the man power, they needed the strength offered by harpoon and lance in order to stress the whale beyond recovery, to siphon the humpback of its will to live and increase the opportunity to kill it by any means, for there was no such thing as a fair go.

The whale was held tight, forced to enter further into the bay where it would meet with death, constantly parried by the killers remorseless strides to heighten the dilemma of the humpback's predicament, savouring the moment when the would gain the upper hand and a mouthful of lip and tongue, the delicacy that they loved so much.

Still fresh of mind and of the ability to perform manoeuvres well, the humpback shifted gear and away from the lurching, snapping jaws of a killer, another chunk of blubber torn from his bulk.

The whale raced for the surface and broke it fast, great volumes of spray pelted here and there, the rowers of a nearby boat smothered from head to foot in cold and dampening hell, the cold of the sea penetrating fast to the bone, stinging at their flesh, numbing the feeling in their hands, toes, and face. But quality is a bequest of any bay whaler and George, young of heart and confident of mind, having been brought up with the knowledge instilled by his father of many years' experience, saw the opportunity provided him and lifted the harpoon above his head in both hands. He thrust down hard at just the right time, where the phosphorus sign of presence pointed to the whale's position both loud and clear, the point of the harpoon penetrating deep, securing itself well within the beast that swam the seven seas.

The 'fast fish' had been secured and Alex Greig's boat, with Fred at the forward thwart with harpoon at the ready, was called to inaction, for the last thing they wanted was for two harpoons to be stuck fast to a single fish, in particular at night when the weather was not sound and it was all the more difficult to keep the boats apart and from smashing each other in impending danger.

Fred Wilson moved to the rear and changed placed immediately with the headsman, John's own boat conducted the same manoeuvre, George moving to the rear and changing places with his father, the lancing of the whale to commence immediately... as soon as it surfaced once again.

The whale had reared its barnacled head at the initial stinging of the harpoon, brought to the reality of the situation as the end commenced to become clear, that he, a humpback of little threat to anyone or anything, other than what could be taken in his mouth and digested within its gut, was being chased down from beneath and above the waves. He was meek, meant no harm, and wished only to move on towards the breeding grounds, to find himself a mate for the season of joy, to pass on his genes at one of the many social gathering of his species upon the face of the world. He sounded immediately on feeling the sting of the harpoon enter his body, diving as deep as he possibly could, the manila rope of the boat dragging out behind him, the rope looped around the loggerhead for ease in control and manipulation, manipulation which did not come easily, although with the help of the pack of killers the men had less to concern themselves with; except the unenviable.

The temperament of a harpooned whale was rather unpredictable, easily pressed into thrashing about in a manner that could not be read by forecast of experience. A harpooned whale was a dangerous animal, as dangerous as they come, the flukes of the animal quite capable of cutting a boat in two.

The ploy of the killers had now changed for the harpoon imbedded within the blubber of the whale meant that lances were to follow. The call went around for the pod to change tactics, the need to press the humpback deeper no longer fitting; they now place all emphasis on keeping the whale as close to the surface as possible.

Tom then leapt from the water, his entire body lifting out of the sea, and he came down hard upon the back of the humpback, sliding upon its blowhole, restricting as best as possible his breathing even for just a few seconds, for all efforts impeded upon the whale to breathe right, think straight, and act with precision upon the predicament he was in. His was growing tired,

tired of the chase, tired of the restrictions imposed upon his abilities, tired from the stress, strain, and overpowering fear.

The whale was forced to remain surfaced, killers either side and one below, the boats now closing in, dragging the line of manila in through the loggerhead, bringing the catch home.

George gave the order to turn towards the whale as he picked up a lance and readied himself against the thigh crunching thwart, steadying himself to unleash his fury, and as the gap was closed between them both he hurled the lance with great precision in the flank of the whale and between the ribs. It penetrated deep and the whale curled in pain, his head lifting out of the water, spray covering the crew once more in salt water and as the particles of moisture drifted quickly away in the wind, to mingle again with the rolling waves, where white crests broke against the unsettled surface.

The humpback endeavoured to sound one more time his flukes lifting out of the water, Alex Greig's boat coming dangerously close to being hammered hard, the downward pressure of the tail's movement creating such a disturbance upon the sea that the boat was pushed rearward, unsettling those on board.

A warning broke the air for all hands to peak their oars, to ready themselves for the fate none looked forward to, preparing themselves to be delivered into the sea with the fury of the whale and the hunger of the killers. No one knew if the killer whales would take the time to chomp on one of them, whether or not they had a taste for man-flesh. None had found the thought a comfort and in particular, none of the men wished to find out.

The tremendous crash came quick and loud but failed to hit anything of concern and the battle continued to be waged with a further two lances breaching the outer skin of the humpback and the 'red flag' flew high and a deafening noise erupted from deep within the whale, a noise so penetrating that it had to be heard to be believed.

When finally the victory was won, the carcass afloat and being mauled by the killers, the whale's mouth being forced open and its tongue eaten hurriedly along with the lips, the crews sat back in exhaustion and looked upon the feeding killers. It was now that George gave the order for a lantern to be lit per each boat, to aid them in their ambition, to provide that little something in order to acquire their desire and need, to assist them in attaching an anchor and for positions within the boats to be changed with ease and control.

The job was done, the fight lasting fifty minutes. The work to anchor the carcass took a little under 45 minutes and no sooner had they finished and the sun decided right then and there to show itself. George's eyes fell upon the biggest humpback he'd ever seen in the bay, dead or alive; it was 15.9 metres long and quite literally dwarfed the boat he was in. This day amongst many others would be remembered by him as the turning point that moulded his life forever, though sculptured in his youth to follow the footsteps of his father from a very early age.

The glamorous side of things had come and gone, the adventure finished with and the hard work to be done; and this by no means should insist that killing a whale was easy, for that would be laughed upon by more than those accommodated with the processes of the fraternity.

The site of the slaying was visited once more, 24 hours after the carcass had been carried by the killers to his watery grave, even if only a temporary place of rest, carried there by Tom and his entourage, the flippers, flukes, and mouth held tight in their mouths, dragged down deep in order to finish with their feeding upon the delicacies so often sought, in particular during the winter months of the east coast of Australia, for their other interests were farther south and currently a contemplation of mind.

The carcass had filled with gases until it floated to the surface, floating upon its side and proving to be very cumbersome, for to drag a whale in when in this position was by far harder to conduct than if it had been floating upright, its back bare to the world above and its underbelly obscured by the salty sea entrapped within the bay.

The anchor was retrieved and the rower's arms bent to the work, the whale being turned in over the bar and to the mouth of the Kiah River, high tide allowing them easier access than if brought in under more severe conditions such as low tide and or bad weather, bringing the prize home and delivering it to the try-works, where capstan and boiling pots awaited its heavenly duty. Boat spades were picked up by the men that had gathered, sharpened points as sharp as could possibly be, the blubber cut into squares with great effort and much sweat, shirt sleeves wiping constantly at the brow and eyes, wiping the salt of the flesh away to reform again.

Seagulls filled the air, brought together by that silent ringing of the dinner bell, to congregate for their opportunity to come, swooping in and pestering the work detail, making a right nuisance of themselves as they always did, squawking that piercing squawk which sounded more and more like the words formed on a drunkards lips, 'mine, mine, mine'. The stench was wretched, beyond belief, uncannily offending and most assuredly the worst

George had the experience in suffering, but to the seagulls it was the perfume of the gods.

The entire process was hard and consuming. First the sheets of blubber were cut from the whale and then turned up the ramp to have further work undertaken upon the blubber, each large portion being cut into strips that were 15 inches x 5 inches x 5 inches deep (as deep as the blubber, most dependent on the size and species of the whale). The strips were cast into a vat; soon after they were minced into smaller portions and boiled within the try-pots. A man then has the duty to skim the surface with a perforated utensil and watched with much attention the boiling take place, ensuring that all went well and that the oil that had been rendered flowed into smaller pots where it was later stored into caskets.

CHAPTER EIGHT

It was a sad time for all. It was 1890, just three short years after George had taken to the boats that Typee and Humpy, birds of a feather, decided to leave the pod. They were to leave behind them a great friend... many great friends in fact, but Stranger was their closest; she was their matriarch, their friend, their strength when times were bad.

It was always the way when breeding season came around; some would leave and others would show, but for the majority of the pod the members always remained the same. Members of their close-knit community were seldom changed by more than a half dozen new saddles patches each year; quite often less. But love would have its way and times change for the worst and the better.

Typee and Humpy would be missed dearly; Typee for his exuberance and will to win over any whale and Humpy for her ability to lead attacks where she would rip chunks of blubber and flesh from lips, flippers and flanks. Her dorsal, the flag of her back, bent completely over and easily recognised by all in the pod, would be sorely missed by all.

The pod gathered around the couple at a place slightly north of the icy coast of the South Pole, resting as they did between attacks on seals and other creatures of the sea, taking the opportunity to rest and sleep a little before their return to Twofold Bay.

Typee and Humpy looked upon the members of their fraternity, their clan, their identity. They stared a deep and longing stare, a submissive look upon their peers that indicated their feelings of remorse, sorrow and apology. Maybe they would one day return but for the time being they wished to endeavour isolation for the wellbeing of their future, to set upon new routines, new feeding habits, new environments for which to bring up their young.

Typee was strong in conviction and was set upon starting a new pod and so with the goodbyes given the pair of killers turned tail and swam away from those that they had come to know so well.

It had been some time now that Typee and Humpy had taken to the ocean on a voyage of discovery and growth when the appearance of another turned the heads of all in the pod.

Stranger was the first to approach the killer whale and had to glance twice before seeing that it was indeed a new saddle patch, but the comparison to Typee was absolutely astounding.

The pod gathered around to introduce themselves as they do with a little vocalisation, skin rubbing and general nosing around. Jackson, the new killer, was quick to accept the offer of dominance handed him, quick looks and broken stares indicating his place in the pod, but nevertheless they were all more than willing to accept him.

It wasn't known where Jackson had come from but he wasn't overly thin so was able to look after himself. He was a stray from somewhere, possibly discarded by another matriarch for disobedient behaviour, or possibly a transient looking for another harbour, one that might offer him better opportunity; he may even have lost a loved one and felt a strong urge to leave the pod of which he was a member. Regardless of his circumstances he fit in well and by the time a return to Twofold Bay was called upon, Jackson, a male of eleven years, saw a resemblance in one of the younger females. She was Sharkey, just two years of age and far from sexual maturity.

At first the attraction wasn't sexual or inappropriate, not at all; it was simply that Sharkey had the appearance and mannerisms of one that Jackson had known in a past life; but the years would unfold and both killers would one day couple, parenting two young of their own, but that was many years away and still nothing more than vapours of mist on a dark horizon.

Jackson fit into place quite quickly and he was accepted rather quickly into the pod. Maybe it was his familiar look, the fact that he resembled Typee that he was taken in with little fuss... or maybe it was his pleasant nature.

CHAPTER NINE

George lances his first humpback, a small animal which provided ample pleasure and confidence; the crew under the 18-year old headsman seeing the man unfold within, aspiration forming like the callous upon a workings man's hand, but the kill was followed immediately by many weeks of frustration as the presence of killers and whales were both equally vacant from the bay.

George and his crew, along with John and his, were sheltered at South Head at the wharf of rock, settled within the cave of substantial size and awaiting the call to action. The weather was fine and it was far easier to put out the boats from the cave, there beneath the shelter of South Head, than to put out from the Kiah Inlet, providing their opposition with the opportunity to move in on a whale when one decided to show.

The men had just polished off lunch and were at rest with mugs of tea tantalizing their senses when a sudden call came from atop the cliff, a whale sighted and followed closely by no less than 6 killer whales.

It was a right whale of large proportions and currently the only fins able to be identified were those belonging to Tom and Hooky. By the time the two boats were cast from the rocky wharf the whale had been well and truly pressured into the mouth of Twofold Bay, Tom and Hooky leaving the mustered whale behind with the remainder of the pod streamlining along on all sides and beneath, keeping the front clear, a path to its demise being cast like the script of a movie.

The two killers recognised for the markings set about swimming around the boats for a short period, as though assessing the situation for what it was worth, John's boat pulling away quite substantially from George's.

Kind and straight forward insults were pressed upon the crews by their respective headsman, verbal assaults of friendly coercion, saw that know-how, self-confidence, and aptitude came boiling to the surface, each man taking control and seeing to it that the oars were employed to their fullest ability, the crews' potential at its peak. The culmination of the combined effort saw the two boats speed off towards their target and the killers that hampered it. It was then that Tom and Hooky, seeing all was faring well, departed the boats and joined the others of their pod in the continuing subjection of their prey.

The right whale was heading straight for John's boat when he ordered for the harpooner to take position, which Alex did with little ado, picking up the metal rod of power and readying himself in position, bracing himself against the thwart and eyeing the whale with suspicion and confirmed action.

George quickly acted upon the situation to his front and moved to the starboard, shifting his position and approach in order to head off what might be a good target, in particular if it surfaced after going beneath his father's boat; but it wasn't to be. The right whale came up quickly, bolstered by the efforts of the killers beneath to bring him up, availing himself as a target to the harpooner for a clear and steady shot. Alex let loose with power in his arm, the harpoon racing through the air to its target, but the moving target was still far out and the shot only imbedded itself just in below the dorsal, a throw that stuck but did not penetrate.

The fish was fast but not overly secure. It could easily, and quite readily, release himself of his encumbrance, to try and flee the scene that had now proved to be a dangerous place, the slight sting bringing coalesced thoughts to mingle within his mind.

Sam Haddigaddi obeyed the order slung in his direction, the friendly suggestion which needn't be called but was made nevertheless. He stood with his harpoon at the ready, to take a shot himself at the back of the right whale, to see if he could do better than Alex, a throw which he had made many times in the past, such experience that had made him a legend of the bay and an asset for the Davidson's, his skill and unwavering commitment given more than praise over the years that had past. He hurled it then as the monster passed them by, hounded by the killers as they took chunks from his sides, another beyond and one further down, the containment holding firm, the whale having nowhere to move. And as the harpoon was hurled towards the right whale the oars were dug into the sea, reversing the shift of the boat, putting a halt to its speedy delivery upon the beasts back.

The line was secure and the loggerhead attended to, water too was poured over it as the line ran out and wood becoming too hot and worrisome. The headsman now changed places with the harpooner, as had already been done on John's boat, two ropes now connected to the whale, two boats now in tow.

John was closer to the whale than George, George being several boat lengths behind his father, both being towed along and unable to do anything about it, the killers doing all they could to muster the great whale, one of the biggest that any of them had seen for quite some time.

The whale had experienced quite enough and was soon heading out to sea, the boats in tow, the killers doing all they could to prevent it from diving more than a few metres, snapping at its heals, biting at its flanks, throwing themselves occasionally upon its back to prevent it breathing properly, but the whale just kept on keeping on, heading further and further from the neck of the bay, out towards the horizon in the east where the sun had already deserted, the last fragrant of light disappearing over the crest of the range around the bay in the west, where their homes beckoned for the men to return, where the warmth of fires and a hot meal could be presented to quench their growing hunger. There was not much for it but to sit back and wait for the whale to tire, for the killers to drag him down, both boats in tow.

The work over the coming time, as the kilometres grew behind them, wasn't hard. Their oars had been peaked and they were being dragged along by the whale. The surf created upon the bows of both boats curled upwards and sprouted out, white crests which commenced to turn phosphorescent as the day became night. It crept upon them rather quickly, not a single star to be seen in the sky, no moon to aid them; the only factor that was currently providing them with any degree of optimism was the fact that the weather, in general, had not turned against them, for although the wind was fresh it was not overall cold and nor was there any rain, drizzle, or water being splashed over them.

Jackets were placed on, more or less at the same time, some a little too small for the wearers, as the men, when first clambering aboard the boats to give chase upon the whale, hadn't taken to quibbling about which boat they were attending. So long as all oars were manned, that was the concern, but now, as the cold commenced to penetrate their bones some of them began to wish that they had their own personal gear to wrap around them, to encase their bodies like a little nut within its shell. This was the case in many circumstances of a hunt, where men found themselves pouring over an oar that was not accustomed to their grip, the portion of an oar which had seen many years of handling worn down by the press of flesh against the grain. It was a little different for harpooners and headsman for they had a command and structure to heed, harpooners hard to come by and employed specifically for the task set them, and headsman... say no more, for a boat was worthless without a leader and someone to hurl the lances – two lancers to a single boat was absurdly useless.

The sign of the whale's intermittent exchange between water haven and surface was made clearer by the phosphorus display before them, the rope in the water also making its mark. The whale was making no sign of giving up, surrender far from its mind. The killers had no way of knowing that they had bitten off more than they could chew when the whale seemed to place himself upon their menu for the day, waltzing comfortably into the bay, being headed off by two boats, two harpoons, and several lances. But the whale had persisted and had turned the power of the play. The land behind them was getting further and further away, and before time they were twelve kilometres out to sea, and their momentum into the darkness didn't waver for a second.

George held his arms tight around him when John's voice broke the noise of the boats being dragged through the water, advising with just anxiousness that the ropes had somehow crossed over and that George needed to cut the line. A sudden upheaval then delivered itself to the air, a thunderous crash which could be none other than one thing and one thing only; the other boat, that of John's, had been hit hard and smashed to pieces. The wrangling of the wreckage reached their ears and Sam leapt to action and with a tomahawk in his hand delivered a blow to the secure line, releasing the boat's connection with the prize that had showered them with its unbelievable courage and fortitude.

The members of the other crew had been cast into the sea, the great whale having turned back on the boat and smashing it hard with its flukes as it sounded and then rose from beneath them, killing Peter Lia immediately, the mass of fluke falling upon him with no warning, the continuing momentum of the downward force splitting the boat into two pieces whereupon it sank.

The mass of wood and lances, tug of manila and thwarts, keg of water and rations; all drift helplessly to the sea floor, including the blond Norwegian who would be remembered always for his happy contemptuous persona and his singing in the try-works where hard labour was always met with a cheerful smile.

The work was now cut out for them and they had to act quickly. The water temperature was cold and too long in the sea would lead to no lack of problems. Cries for help appeared from out of nowhere, the black surrounds enveloping all, a little phosphorus providing assistance into where someone was splashing, treading water, or swimming precariously towards the only boat afloat, the only item of worth that the surviving eleven men had between them and Twofold Bay.

A few of the killers then separated from the remainder of the pod to undertake a different task, a task which went unnoticed by those in the water or at safe harbour in their little green boat.

Under the command of Cooper; Big Ben, Tom, Hooky, Jackson, Sharkey and Jimmy, took positions around the scene to protect and serve. It was clear to the killers that they were far out to sea and that sharks would be in the vicinity. The last thing Stranger or any of the others wished was for their allies to be picked off by hungry mouths which in turn would diminish their ability to maintain energy levels as they currently experienced as an unmistakable advantage in their survival.

One by one the men were drawn out of the water, drenched completely, utterly and miserably cold, the chill of the sea having sapped them completely of all energy, depriving them of everything except their spirit to live and the thoughts they had for their friend Peter.

And the ring around the boat afloat was maintained during the ordeal and once all of the men were secured the killing was continued, a return to the excitement of the fray pitting all the killer whales to frenzy.

The gunwale of the boat was just centimetres from the surface of the sea, so dangerously close to being sunk by a surge of water. The only thing that saved the day was the fact that the sea was as calm now as it was when the sun at disappeared over the horizon, taking with it their ability to see. Nothing at all could be seen. Individuals had been plucked from the sea, guided by voice and phosphorus. One by one they were pulled from the chill of the water, taken into safety, their friends pleased to see them alive.

Positions within the boat were quickly taken up, each and every one taking turns at the oars, those that were dry assuring their comrades that they would draw enough water to have them safely ashore soon enough and those drenched to the bone readying themselves for a turn in order to warm themselves as best they could, to hold the cold at bay.

Instinct now took command and the coast was made for, land which could not be seen, not a light upon the shores of the bay evident whatsoever.

After many hours of stroking the oars upon the watery grave they came upon the sound of surf hitting the coastline and not long after the sighted their first real break... Jim was on South Head with a lantern in his hand, waiting as patiently as he possibly could for their return, and then they drew into the bay, eleven men in bad shape, some worse off than others.

None would forget this day, the worst day that any of them could remember. Peter Lia was lost; a boat was lost; a whale had made clear its intension and had either made it safely away from the killers with harpoons still attached, or being eaten as the men pulled the boat ashore; either way they were not going back to find out. In memory of their loss an inscription was cast into the stone of Boyd's Tower, dated September 28th, 1881; to Peter Lia, who was killed by a whale.

CHAPTER TEN

Tom and the others had broken off their quest to catch the fin whale, a hazardous fight with so few killers available, for something had caught their attention; they were coming up from the rear of the grand steamer, the SS Ly-ee-Moon as it made its way towards Sydney.

She was a steamer of great prestige and held in high esteem, for when she was built she was one of the fastest at 17 knots and furnished with only the best that money could buy, initially built as a paddle steamer in 1859, a ship which measured 86 metres long and 8.2 wide, powered by a coal fed steam engine which turned the huge wheels. She was originally rigged with three masts and fitted with sail and could make good speed where weather permitted, but times change and within 20 years (1878) was returned to service after being modified by the removal of a mast and turned into a schooner-rigged vessel.

There were few lights on board and all seemed quiet, the ship plodding along at a leisurely pace and all on board completely unaware as to what lay ahead.

She'd departed Melbourne on Saturday 29 May with 55 passengers and a crew of 41. Captain Webber had left control of the vessel in the care of the Third Officer, James Fotheringhame, at 7.45 pm, a man of great worth and handed much respect over the years. They were approaching Gabo Island with the lighthouse of 3 years in full sight. The lighthouse was 29 metres high, 44 metres above sea level, and sat upon the crest of the land and able to be seen at distances of up to 18 kilometres.

The killers of Cooper's pod escorted the ship and it made its way over the gentle rollers, white surf thrown up from the bow, the sound of the sea wasted upon the night so young; Gabo Island was growing bigger in the window and Fotheringhame fought better of his abilities and considered his position before making a hasty decision, for the captain had retired most definitely and wasn't to be disturbed until nearing Green Cape at 26 kilometres south of Twofold Bay. Unbeknown to Fotheringhame the captain was snug within his cabin, suckling on a bottle, getting rather drunk.

Tom could see as he spy hopped a little, how a man departed the bridge and made his way down towards the rear of the ship, throwing waste into the sea from the stern, unaware of the killers as they swam without a care in the world. It was at this point that Fotheringhame made the hasty decision to call upon the services of the captain, for him to be called to duty, but the captain flatly refused to attend the bridge.

Time and time again over the next hour, Fotheringhame saw to it that he pestered the captain as he believed was his duty until the constant calls for him to return to the bridge got the better of him and he attended with a huff and eyes full of scorn, filled with alcohol and not giving a damn for Fotheringhame's urgent need.

It was now 9 pm and the captain's return quickly saw to it a little soberness enter his otherwise blunted views and from there upon the bridge could plainly see the rocks of Green Cape growing through the windows of the bridge and ordered engines to be reversed, but he was too late and the ship hit rocks. Tom and the others could not foresee the danger as it pressed ever forward, unlike the captain with his years of mounted experience, and within two minutes she broke in two, the stern upon the reef and the bow floating precariously towards the shore.

The dangerous predicament was an accident out of all proportion, the rocks at the base of Green Cape most dangerous and offering nothing at all in regards to cushioning the blows of flesh upon them; but the fight for survival commenced in a rush where adrenalin took place over clear thinking.

The lighthouse workers heard the commotion, the grinding of the ship, the thrashing of it against the rocks, Daniel Whelan and George Walters coming to the assistance of those in dire need. They were alerted well to the unforgivable sea, where wood was superficial when compared against the jagged edges of rock and cliff.

Tom and the others of the pod in which he was a member moved in, but not too close, for even with their skill and experience of the sea, the rocks proved to be treacherous and unyielding.

The foremast upon the bow fell and landed upon rock where seamen and others started to crawl to safety, a fishing line then thrown to the ship on which was attached a rope. With the rope tied fast the first of the passengers, Herbert Lumsdaine, made for the safety of the shore with the help of the lighthouse workers, swinging beneath the rope as it swayed; Andrew Bergland, a passenger, along with Fotheringhame, also made it to safety along with a further 10 people including Ola Thorpe, the boatswain, and the captain, who was last to leave the ship, the only duty he performed admirably this night. Amongst the survivors was Mrs Flora Hannah MacKillop, an elderly lady, mother of the Mother Superior of St Joseph's Provident Institution; mother to Mary MacKillop.

Tom takes to the scene, trying to rescue some that are clinging near the rocks, but they fear for their lives, not knowing what Tom is or what he is trying to attempt – their salvation. He swims in as close as he possibly dares and then away again, giving up on the hopeless situation, as he is thrust against a formation of large rock, a large piece of his jaw and several teeth being knocked out, a scar for life that would tell his tale of courage for ever and a day. He retreats having secured no victory, for it was too treacherous, even for him.

It is then that further screaming continues unabated and for the remainder of the night 20 persons can be heard crying out for help, all aboard the stern which is washed further out to sea.

The killers move in under the directions of Tom, and although he is not the leader of the pod, what he has to say is most important. A rescue attempt must be staged, in similarity to what they would do for those within the green boats of Twofold Bay... the Davidson's and their crew. He can remember quite clearly how the man, Peter Lia, was killed by the flukes of the whale gone mad and how the body sank lifelessly towards the bottom of the sea, the visual picture clear in his mind.

Again the killers attempted to move in and help those aboard, trying in all their effort to grasp the people's attention, to help them to safety where possible, to provide protection from the hungry mouths of the sea, to do justice where justice should be served. The Davidson's had served them well over the years and in return they should do the same, for the society of humans was as much a part of their pod as they were of theirs. Like brothers and sisters they were intelligent and emotional, showed semblance in many respects, but still they feared the worse... the people did not jump to salvation but allowed themselves to be dragged under the waves, fighting off the killers where one strayed too close.

And so many lives were lost unnecessarily, 71 to be exact, three of which were very young children; and the killers swam off as the sun rose above the horizon, swimming towards Leatherjacket Bay, to head off a whale that they had heard swimming in the waters the night before, and although the monster fish was too large for them alone there was the distinct possibility that other members of their community would happen along sooner rather than later, for the pods were to congregate for further fishing near Twofold Bay, to assist in the killing of whales as the season fell upon them over the coming weeks. A surprise was also awaiting them.

Humpy had returned to the pod she had known so well, returned with her son, Walker, who was barely one year old.

It seemed strange that she should return alone, but it was not possible for Humpy to portray the tragedy that unfolded during a clash with a humpback whale and calf. Typee had taken a fluke directly in the side which was enough to split him open, an uncommon and freak occurrence. He died some time after... Humpy had no real choice but to return to the Eden pod, leaving behind her fond memories and the estranged community of other killers that had pegged her at the bottom of the chain, treating her with defiance rather than showing gratitude for her skilled and athletic hunting ability.

Humpy's years away from home were a reflection of her mind she cared little to remember. Other than the fact that Typee would never be seen again the years away from Stranger was a time she didn't wish to recall. Walker was also accepted and looked after as any other young mouth; as a true member of the family that evolved around him.

CHAPTER ELEVEN

By the 1890s, George Davidson, or Fearless George as he was known, took over the family business, relying on ingenuity to survive from year to year where vegetable gardens, chicken runs, fishing and livestock were a part of everyday life, in particular the off season. But where winter was waited upon so the rewards were set, and when the reward was close to shore there was fighting to be done.

When the fighting had been done and a victory secured the crew would tie an anchor and buoy to the dead mass which sank quite quickly, it was then that the killers took great joy in feeding on the baleen by eating the tongue and lips only as was usual. In around 24 hours, give or take, enough gas would build up in the dead whale to such a degree that the prize would float to the surface; it was now that the bay whalers would row out and tow back the reward of their patience and collaboration, back to the try-works on the banks of the Kiah River.

The relationship between the two species continued to evolve and whenever a killer became tangled in ropes a rescue attempt would be set into motion, a just reward for the protection the killers had offered in the past by protecting the crews from sharks if the green whaleboats were smashed and torn apart. Serious accidents were numerous, but rarely fatal. But of all the things that had evolved there was one that will always be remembered, and that was the incident of the painter.

Several killers had ventured into the bay, to give warning to the men ashore, that a humpback was within reasonable distance and ready for the taking. Two other pods were taking all the normal precautions except the distance between the pods was drastically reduced. It was a big fish and required extra hands to impede on its efforts to get far out to sea where the ability to dive could strip the killers of all advantage, placing great stress upon their combined effort, to force a victory over those that pressed home the attack.

Tom lead the way and all three commenced flop-tailing, jumping from the water and then hitting it hard, the unmistakable calling travelling far and wide, a beacon to holdfast the interests of a whaling man, to call him to duty, to express without any doubt that there was a whale to be had but it would not wait all night. And from the dark depths of the whalers cabin, where men lay asleep, dreams filling the few that had not partaken of any alcohol (or less than the norm), came that call which shred the anxiousness from men stricken with the fear of going an entire season without as much as seeing a single whale.

RUSHO!

Unmistaken in its sound and shrill; unmistaken in it command and call to duty; unmistaken in the offerings ahead if they were to be successful in securing another kill.

There had been a heavy night of the spirits, only a handful of men available, and capable, of filling the positions within a single boat, a boat which George took under his command, giving the words as appropriate to extricate more power, for each occupant to heave his arms to the task at hand, to hit the sea hard with each stroke and pull with all their might the oars under their charge.

George looked carefully towards the heavens above, as a student would study his books before compiling his work, looking to the hours which lay ahead, to understand the situation as it was now and as it would be in several hours from now. As it stood there was a half moon and sparse cloud was making its way across the sky, a westerly breeze blowing strong, but the sea appeared quite calm. By all appearances they were in for an easy night where the sea was concerned; but what of the whale?

Rising from the darkness the rowers then heard the familiar sound of a humpback whale in the midst of its dilemma, it being hounded by the pods a little further out to sea, and the killers could clearly hear the presence of the beats, the oars pounding the sea.

Tom remained at the stern of the boat, having gained the men's attention and leading the way, phosphorus showing the direction to follow when the light from the moon took to hiding behind the occasional cloud, the bond with their friends of the sea instilling great confidence and satisfaction.

Tom came then to the side of the boat, understanding as he did that time was of the essence and in this case, more so, for there was only one boat to do the task of which would normally go to two or three, hard work ahead which required great masses of stamina. He sideswiped the boat gently from beneath, oars pushed aside, which drew the obvious attention of the whalers as they rowed, dark eyes falling upon the mass, to where the dorsal stretched out from the sea and towards the sky, a fin which was enormous and struck them all with a little fear: it showed itself as possessing empowerment and stability.

Queries were passed around between breathes as the boat pressed ever forward, questions on the aggressive behaviour and the possibility that the boat could be pushed over, and they all in the sea and thrashing to stay afloat. They were trying to row the boat and were being hampered, their progress affected drastically. And the then one of the seated declared a solution, Tom Earl allowing a little chuckle to escape his lips as he suggested that they throw him a rope, the painter at the bow.

George looked inquisitively upon the suggestion and saw that Tom was growing anxious, seemingly annoyed at their progress, and beneath the waves, as Tom sped along, he feared the humpback would make its escape and the youngest of the pod would not survive the winter, for they were all hungry but currently preferred to remain at Twofold Bay, for the aid provided them by the men and their sticks of iron did much in keeping at bay the dissension within their group, where mothers were concerned for their young; but one good whale could change all of that and provide them with enough sustenance to carry them on until the next kill.

The killer hit the flank again, oars in danger of being lost, and George gave the command for the harpooner to throw the painter in the water, to see what Tom would do with the rope, to see for himself if this killer whale was up to no good or trying emphatically to provide them with assistance.

The quizzical look upon the harpooner's face drew a collection of eyeballs, each clicking into position as the fell upon the dark man, the oar lifted most temporarily from the water and the painter reached for, thrown into the sea with very little effort, and the oar put into motion one more time.

Jaws dropped instantaneously and the forward motion of the boat slowed dramatically as Tom opened his mouth and allow the rope to fall into place before the bellowing voice of the headsman brought them back to reality. Tom was pulling them through the water, aiding them as best he could, the first time ever that a killer whale, or any mammal for that matter, had allowed himself to aid a human upon the undulated waters of the planet earth.

This was a scene to remember, one for the books, an incident that would never be forgotten by that experiencing it, and the two killers that were with Tom looked upon the manner of his action and tried with all their effort to understand it, for there was no immediate reason why Tom would be doing such a thing, for this was no time for play, this was no time for fun; there was work to be done, and a lot of it. And then it hit them, the boat was making good headway now, better than before, the men rowing as hard as before, with true conviction encompassing them all and Tom was assisting them with an ingenious method that was simply absurd; but yet it worked. But how was it achieved, what had Tom done to procure the rope?

Whistles, clicks and calls filled the ocean around. The expanse around was a-buzz with the noise of echolocation clicks, both isolated and in trains, the nasal passages beneath their blowholes created upheaval amongst the killers. The pods combined repertoire of calls was quite large in number, around 23 employed by Tom and his immediate family, both immediate and secondary, some sounds made at times of chasing down a whale, others for directing signals and commands to particularly pods; other signals and signs were used extensively for reaping harvest and reward; as well as this there was a call that distinguished one killer from another, a name that identified a particular individual where distance was an issue.

The sonic signatures of the acoustic communication consisted of pitch, loudness, harmonic structure, tone, urgency, mood, and action; all aided in understanding and enabled the killers to perform tasks that complimented their every movement. Sometimes they employed singular clicks as opposed to click trains and this depended largely on the type of prey they were hunting. Marine mammals would pick up quite easily on the clicks of the killers, but fish could not. Passive listening was simply an extension of their ability to sound commands and requests. Calls to indicate strategies, prey species, and pod members; that's all that was needed, that's all there was.

The very effort and commotion of the fight to keep the whale at bay was doubled in all its constituted values, the boat nearing its final approach, the whale, too, trying with one last gigantic effort to get away from the pods, turning upon the teeth infested mouths with herculean effort surfacing its raging scorn, strength erupting like a volcano from its sinew as energy was eaten up at an alarming rate in order to secure an escape. But escape would be hard to win for a humpback could only muster 12 kilometres an hour, where the killer could do up to 30 kilometres an hour – but rarely travelled more than 160km a day.

Tom dropped the rope which was ignored for the time, the importance of the game growing clear to their front, the escort of three killers joining in the final fray where the humpback came towards the boat.

The harpooner got ready in an instant, seeing the large mass of black coming full steam from the front, the gap closing fast between the two. The headsman grasped the steering oar with both hands and pulled it into his chest as he leant back, the boat moving to the side and the whale coming up parallel. The harpooner stood then, cloud moving in front on the moon most temporarily, and then with the sudden realization that a clear target was available the harpooner struck out hard with the iron in his hand.

The harpooner, with more luck than could be afforded the situation, released a good throw that penetrated deep and stuck well; the 'fast fish' was made. The whole issue of fight and slander had worked to a means and their purses could feel the colour of money before the try-pots could smell the blubber of the carcass just won.

The humpback reared its slim head, though broad and rounded when seen from the top, a rounded protuberance beneath the tip of the lower jaw, fleshy knobs of barnacle covering most of its head, spouting clear from its blowhole, the water vapours void of that reddish tinge so often sought, which flew two metres into the air in bushy contrast, thrashing from side to side and its back commencing to arch, the flukes coming up towards the surface in preparation to dive, a small dorsal fin two-thirds down its back: a nubbin of little consequence. He was black with white around the throat and belly; the flippers too were white underneath but darker on top.

Water fell upon them from beneath the crushing flukes, a convex shaped surge of surf that disassociated itself from the molecules of the sea, a separate entity with one concern and one concern only, to drench those within the boat, to soak the wearers of jacket and shirt to the very core.

Gasps of shock erupted from their mouths as the cold of the water hit home, the stabbing of the ocean's dousing driving home the horrors of the sea at its mildest, and lucky they all were that the boat did not go under and stillness came over the sea, for the whale and the killers had disappeared from sight. Several men surrendered their oars and quickly emptied the boat of what water could be found in the bottom before once again returning to their duty.

The surface then erupted once more and the body masses of all involved surfaced again; the harpooner then changed positions with the headsman, lancing to commence immediately. All of a sudden silence fell over them again and for a brief second or two there was nothing but the cloud in the sky, the moon and its light, and the sea and its stabbing cold.

By the time George had taken to the stern the fighting amongst the two species of whale had culminated with great chunks of blubber being torn from the humpback, but the fight below the surface was far from being won. The humpback was heading further out to sea, making for an escape from the smaller-than-usual pod. Again they surfaced and the oars were pulled back in bursts of fury.

In many cases, if not all, the killers would rally together when their prey had been trapped within the bay or it was evident that the whale in question was securing a victory by escaping into open water. This was such a scenario and as the predicament became more than clear the killers swarmed in from all sides in a frantic effort to kill the whale once and for all.

As the green boat continued to maintain its visual connection with the fight, the harpoon still secure, the killers did all they could to hamper the escape. Killers were throwing themselves upon the blowhole, others were snatching on tight to the lips in order to prevent the humpback from sounding, and others continued to rip chunks from its bulk and take bites from the fins. In another effort to throw the assault into affray the humpback dived and turned, the line between boat and harpoon falling slack, and the order to counter the turning beast was shrieked out loud for all to hear but it came too late. The movement of the rope and boat had caught George's leg and into the clam sea he toppled, the stabbing cold knocking the wind out of him like never before. Sam and Albert sprang to life and commenced to cut the line free, for the humpback had returned to the stern and was heading further out to sea, pulling them away from where George had gone under.

For what seemed an eternity the headsman was being dragged beneath the surface of the sea, alongside the boat in tow, but seconds later he shook himself free and released himself of the weight of his shoes and jacket, working himself quickly to the surface where the light of the moon brought great relief, but for a short second only, for the boat was more than four football fields away by the time the line could be cut and the men able to return to rescue their captain.

The solace of the sea in those few minutes shook the very foundations of George as he tread water in order to stay afloat... sharks! Cowards they were, one and all, scared to life of the killer whales but would come running to the party as though gathering to the sound of a dinner bell, drawn by the action of the fight and torments of the whale, to sup themselves upon the carcass once the killers had had their way with the humpback, ready to devour what they could of the meal before it was wasted to the sea grave far below. And where could one find more sharks than out to sea, far from the encumbrance of the shore, where trouble was brewed from their gatherings and misdemeanours of the sea.

George could feel their presence, he was sure of it, as sure of that feeling as anything else in his life to date. And then it came upon his ears, the swirling of the sea, the disturbance of the surface, the sound which pushed dread and surmounting fear into his fragile shell, for he could be no more at risk than as he was at present; by himself and far out from shore, no boat by his side and no knife to ward off an intruder of the dark passages of the waters about him.

His eyes popped from his skull as the view of the fin came to surface, heading towards him on a slight angle, the unmistakable mast of a shark on the prowl. But what was this?

More fin rose above the surface of the sea, far too much for it to be a shark, and the knob atop the fin... it was Tom. But this didn't release the dread and terror from Fearless George for the killers were more menacing than the sharks. If a shark feared the killer then the killer was the most feared of all. No shark ever interfered with the joys of a killer whale as it played and fed upon its victims. This killer whale before him, Tom the killer whale whom he had come to know so well from the safety of his green boat, was about to snack on him, take him within his jaws and crunch him like a peanut beneath his foot.

Many times had George seen a killer take on a shark and win; many times – more than any man could imagine – had he seen them take on a whale that was so enormous by comparison that it was beyond all belief; imagine what it could do to him. And Tom looked upon the form of the man, seeing George close up and personal, seeing the man bobbing there, up and down, a salmon ready for the taking. George stared back, watching the beast as it

100

closed the gap even more and swam around him, George turning on the spot, not daring to take his eyes from the killer had had come to know so well. He tried to console himself then, that the killer known as Tom would not trouble him, that he would be left alone... he didn't wish to be toyed with, thrashed about like a plaything before being drawn into the throat of a killer whale.

The minutes ticked by and the boat from which George had been thrown came out of the darkness and the moon above released itself from the clouds in the sky.

Tom was still circling and George saw friendship in his eye. The boat drew alongside and pulled George to safety, wrapping him in a blanket as quickly as they could. George maintained the visual on Tom and Tom nodded his head as though in friendly gesture before turning into the task ahead and returning to fight the whale with the remainder of his pod.

The experience was unbelievable; this great monster of the sea was as friendly as a lap cat. Tom meant George no harm; he had in fact surrendered himself to the protection of George until such a time that he could be rescued by the others. Tom was indeed a good friend and if it wasn't for him, George would have been taken by a shark.

Tom had returned to his pod under Cooper, looking briefly upon Big Ben, Jackson, Jimmy and Albert. Cooper easily recalled how they had protected the men before by encircling them in a protective case of flesh, but Tom had taken it to the next level. It seemed nothing more than stupidity to get so close to the men when danger was looming and all was tense. They could easily be seen as a threat and had seen men act against them before. Tom could easily have been mistaken for a danger and skewered well by the lance of a man upon the green boat, put in his place once and for all.

Tom couldn't understand the unfamiliarity for they had all experienced nothing more than great salvation from the men. The men served them well by providing food, allowing them 'first rights' to lip and tongue, giving them sustenance as an offering or reward just as the Yuin had done for Stranger in years past.

Tom had laid the last of the questions upon the foundation of understanding. The men and the killers now seemed to have a better understanding of one another. The bond between them was now secured as strong as it could ever be and it would never break.

CHAPTER TWELVE

The following year, 1901, only nineteen killer whales returned: Humpy, Stranger, Cooper, Big Ben, Tom, Hooky, Jackson, Sharkey, Jimmy, Big Jack, Walker, Young Ben, Albert, Brierly, Youngster, Skinner, Kinscher, Charlie Adgery, and Little Jack. The group were split amongst three main pods, Stranger (as matriarch), Hooky and Cooper being sub-pod leaders.

The humpback population would receive a reprieve this year for they were still numerous in number and although easy picking for such a fine pod, all know, there is safety in numbers. And there was an obscure clue to the dwindling numbers of the killers, and it had nothing to do, whatsoever, with a food shortage. The Norwegians whalers were in Australian waters and shooting, quite openly, killer whales as they swam harmlessly about, and this was clarified by the numerous reports of Norwegians boasting, quite recklessly, of their poor behaviour upon the sea. They were concerned that the killers would eat the whales that the whalers caught, hence taking money from their pockets. It was a demoralising dilemma to see that the traits of human ignorance had the effect that it did; even the Yuin people were moving away from Eden and with it a great pool of hard workers which would be sorely missed.

The Davidson's use of oared boats, as opposed to motor boats, continued to favour them in regards to their friendship with the killers, the pod returning year after year. It wasn't so much as a requirement to survive, for now after so many years of collaboration and showing of affection (which completely dissimilar to touches and strokes) they simply wished to cooperate with the crews of the green boats for the pleasure of the chase, the thrill of the kill, the satisfaction of being so sacredly formed with a human that walked the crust of the earth instead of swimming within its waters. But during the final stages of the Davidson's enterprise, where bay whaling was starting to die out due mainly to the cost of effort and falling value of oil, the crews were drawn to a friend named J.R.Logan who would quite happily tow their rowboats out to sea, to deliver them within reach of a corralled baleen, by use of his yacht the 'White Heather'.

The use of silent and effective hand-thrown harpoon and lance were still employed, for the cooperation of the pod was needed now more than ever, and if it should be said then let it be said now, that the whales felt more affection for the crews than the crews did for them until such a time that mournful memory of the past would come back to haunt the dreams of all those that hunted with the killer whales for around 90 years: which occurred at the time of Tom's passing and was still far, far away.

CHAPTER THIRTEEN

The passing of a relative and friend is poorly accepted, none more-so than the death of George's father, where memories of the great man came flooding back over the pursuing days and nights, where dreams were filled with the laughter and fighting spirit of the one called Dad. It was 1903 and John Davidson was dead.

It is the bond between father and son, a bond which can be thicker than that between a mother and her siblings, but a bond that is so seldom celebrated. Whaling was a tough business and a tough business builds tough character, a character which often hides the pains of death and fails to reflect the love that one feels. But George wasn't afraid to show his feelings, in particular amongst his family... but the job of hunting must continue and so the reflections of a special bond is held back for personal rumination and the green boats of Twofold Bay once again become the apparatus for which to deliver their prowess.

George looked over the men in the boat as they rammed the bow into the little surf that sprang up before them, breaking upon the sleekness of their tool-of-the-trade. He lapsed most temporarily upon his father and then saw the characters of those to the front of him leap out of their skins. Another boat could be heard as it too entered the water with a thud.

The men before him, stroking the sea with their oars as only they knew how, their backs facing him as he steered from the stern, were men of adventure, men of the sea, men one-and-all. Most were becoming old men, not just in years but also through the tally of years, where mounting hard-yakka piled on the age in double helpings, two serves for one. Charlie, Archer (George's brother) and Boyd (not to be confused with the opposition) were rather long in the tooth but for the most part George could not be more satisfied with those that manned the boats: Sam, Bert, Peter and Albert Thomas, Harry, Bobbo, Dan, and of course, Alex Greig.

And from the corner of his eye he caught glimpses of shadow, noises from afar reached his ear, his senses heightened and he peruses the shores and bay around him, looking intently for those of the competition... Boyd and Glover. Both were as keen as he to see a 'fast fish' secured, each had crews with ambition and the power to press upon an oar more fatigue than could possibly flow through their own pores, for there was more strength in character, persistence, and ambition than there was in the strength of muscles, sinew, and tissue.

Glover could be seen from the flank, but slightly back and behind George and his two boats. The competition was lacking this morning but that didn't allow for anyone to slacken off; not for a second. Anything could happen... an oar might snap, a man could be thrown – or fall – into the water, or the whale could simply change tactics and come up at the bow of Glover's boat, giving him the opportunity of a lifetime. If there was one thing that had been learnt, it was that the killers and their prey were unpredictable, even with the killer's cooperation.

The men continued to lean into the work, their backs breaking as they asserted their efforts, their muscles tearing from lean to pulp in order to grow in power and strength. This was regimen of instilled action, a commandeering action learnt over many years where it was impossible to know how many days or weeks would elapse between each opportunity for the men to show their grit and fortitude; but still their solid builds, each hardened like steel, dealt out all that could be given.

With sudden realisation and the clarity of the chase racing back to their minds in flashes of black and splashes of sea upon them and their boats, the humpback burst from the horrors of the sea and lifted almost entirely out of the water, only the flukes remaining attached as though by some sacred umbilical that provided sanctuary and peace of mind. It came crashing upon the sea then, a killer erupting from below the surface of the sea, throwing himself upon the back of the baleen, and the horror struck faces of the men in the green boats followed the action of the chase as it unfolded before their very eyes.

Orders to the rowers were issued in calmness and with ease, in loud bellows that were surely heard over the theatre of war, of that which was unfolding around them. But some of the men were haphazardly slow and several oars bore the brunt of the whale gone crazy, where thrashing of body and fluke, as she passed them by under full steam of the chase.

Sam Haddigaddi poised for less than a millisecond before thrusting his harpoon with all the power that he could muster and the iron rod of death departed his callused hand as the oars snapped like toothpicks, Sam thinking briefly that he had somehow broken an arm with the power of the throw.

The squelch of the point entering the whale went unnoticed by all around, all but the whale that bore the brunt of the throw; for him the noise went raking across him and cascaded down his back, deafening to say the least. Every throw was the same, no matter what the species of whale. Every whale in every ocean of the world heard and felt the same, the heart-wrenching threat of Death calling for death. The agony of knowing was the worst as the whale continued to fight the fight which would not be won. The sinking of the great leviathan was swamped at that instant, drowned in the torment that man had aided the death blows of the killers of the sea. What had he done to man to deserve such foul treatment?

But fight he did and it continued with a spurting of energy, a coalesced force of supernatural energy that burst from all its pores and with the curtain drawing to a close the whale raced towards the face of the cliff that overhung the sea. It then turned with one final attempt of escape, melee being entered, killers in the fray and the boats of men close behind. It was no good; the channel to freedom was open to the humpback. He turned again towards the cliff and sped off with the powerful thrashing of its flukes, the killers feeling within them that now were the time to finish the whale once and for all.

With all suddenness the humpback disappeared under the water and the green boat turned as though upon a merry-go-round. The whale began to surface with the boat upon its back, the men jostling for a hold upon the fragile shell that surrounded them. The head of the whale began to surface and the boat too. George jumped to his feet without second thought and leapt forward, landing upon the whales back. Within seconds flat he pushed hard upon the stern of the boat with the power invested within his legs and the boat began to swing to sea; he leapt again, this time back towards the boat, clinging to the safety of his beloved and scrambled to victory. The looks upon the men spoke more than words and for the briefest of moments the entire world sang out loud that the name Fearless George had true meaning. The chase then continued.

The demise of their situation finally bit hard when the humpback refused to fall victim of the whims of both killers and man. A last ditch effort was made once more. The instinct to survive was strong within the humpback and it was up to the killers to bring the final demise to fall upon the mass of blubber at it tried to escape the snapping jaws of those around him, and with one last ditch effort the killers forced, undeniably, the humpback upon the rocks near South Head where the last breaths of life were confused in rapid action, panic and torment having taken its toll. The whale was dead.

It was a sad state of affairs for both man and beast who had secured the victory, for the carcass was going nowhere; out of reach of the killer's mouths and in difficult surrounds for the securing of blubber. There was no need to anchor and buoy the carcass, no wait for the gases to have its affect upon the mass of flesh and bone, for the easy access to the blubber – the usual means by which they secured their pay – had not been denied them all. But what God gives with one hand he takes with the other and in respect to this the dilemma is surely realised, for the whale was going nowhere, literally... they would not even be able to tow it into harbour and then the try-works. The mass would have to be deblubbered where it lay, upon the rocks of the shore, from beneath the cliff where the afternoon sunshine never struck, where blasts from a westerly wind lashed out relentlessly. It was here, amongst the rocks and the surf, where the waves thrashed out upon the legs of the men, their stability drowned like the sorrows of a drunkard on a barroom stall. It was here, amongst the dangers of the sea and coast that the men had to suffer their burden and do all they could to muster the appropriate will to conquer all fear and work their fingers to the bone.

The men, on occasion, looked out and over the sea, where the swells from further out began to crest higher and higher, where the weather began to turn sour and fill itself with scorn. They all knew well that they had several hours of work ahead but they did not know how long it would be before the heavens opened up upon them and the current crashing of waves upon the rocky outcrop of their demoralising station grew in ferocity and lashed out in anger. It was as though there was a god that lived amongst the waves, a titan of gigantic power and skill, Poseidon by name and by justice, for they had taken a creature from the sea, forced it ashore from its garden of Eden, to slash at its body, to cut away its life in chunks and strips, for it to be melted down within pots before being stored in barrels and readied for market. And Alex Greig thanked God that he wasn't Greek.

And far out from shore the killers congregated and swam around in circles, annoyed to the hilt that a meal of sustenance had been denied them. The men weren't to blame; they knew this; and neither was it the fault of the sea. It was the damn whale, having beached itself upon rocks, rocks that cut easily into the thick skin of any animal of the sea, the rocks buttresses and sharp edges cutting relentlessly, sawing at the flesh as the sea rolled the embodied mass up and down, a slab of meat upon a butcher's chopping board and being hacked at mercilessly.

The killers gave to spy-hopping and watched the men work their skill at securing the catch as best they could. Tools had been ferried from the try-works and the carving had begun, the upperside worked on feverishly, the underside a bloody mess where oil from the blubber caked the rocks and sheaves of white adorned the area. There was much urgency in their quest and Tom could see quite easily how the men's attention was drawn to the sea on occasion; not to look at them but to maintain a watching eye upon the storm as it commenced to wonder in; and with the storm came another opportunity, for a call was then received further out, a whale was bypassing their position, a sperm whale with calf further out to sea, an uncommon occurrence which grew in popularity, the offering of good veal crossing their path less and less as the years rolled by. This 'was' to be blamed on man for his relentless pursuit had seen to it that the sperm whale was becoming less common in the waters of the world to such a degree that it was seldom sought. But the calf; that would have to be taken, for joy of taste; for the joy of the chase.

The signal came again, the calf being of reasonable size. The pack of killers would do well to swim the extra distance, and although the sperm and her calf were on a course which led them away from the pack, they were sure to catch up in no time at all, to be able to return to Twofold Bay by morning's first light... if the killing went well.

One last signal then came from where the sperm lay, to cease with all further communication, to continue the hunt in silence. The whale and her calf had been drawn to the localisation of the killer whales but they did not know that they meant to commence a chase for the purpose of feeding. To the whale there was no real concern, for the killers were so far away, yet she would maintain an open ear to the goings on, to ensure the purpose of her and the calf remained solid, that their quest to warmer waters for feeding purposes could be secured. The Hawaii Islands were a long way off but she knew the waters well, knew of great abundances of food at this time of year. With their attention turned again to the path ahead they continued unabated.

The shadows of the noise around them, the movement of the sea and other creatures of the ocean, all gave to the accumulative effect which helped to masquerade their move. The killers were on the hunt, dangerous and hungry, meaning to deliver their combined skills, to sink their teeth into the best blubber around, to rip at the calf in manipulative action before setting their sights upon the female of the species. It wouldn't be easy for the female would hinder their moves, give her all to secure the survival of her young, but try as she might the killers would win their prize and get their fill.

By the time Tom and the others were feeding upon the calf the men upon the rocks had completed their task, had set their oars into the waters and not before time, for the weather commenced to grow in its ferocity once more, mounting waves of surging white crashing with great intent upon the place where the humpback's remains were washed into the sea for the smaller fish to have their way, for crab to take their share, for seagulls to make their move. But the move would be delayed shortly until after the storm and by then it might be too late, so the creatures moved in immediately and made the most of the little time they had.

CHAPTER FOURTEEN

The proprieties of bay whaling were appalling in 1904, and from one year to the next the ambitions of many men were dashed by the infrequent appearance of whales, whether they be minke or fin. It costs money, and plenty of it, to run a bunkhouse full of men, several boats and a household with wife and siblings. It is true that idleness breeds discontent but where Twofold Bay and the community were concerned, in particular those that had trouble rubbing butter upon the face of their bread, discontent wasn't accompanied by the inappropriate, mismanaged husbandry of fellowship and personal discipline.

Although drink was permitted it wasn't something easily afforded, but gambling was an inbred vacuum which sucked the pockets dry. What one man wins one week he loses in another, but pay was seldom offered until the oil and bone was sold. So when the time comes for the call to be made, rousing itself from the roll of the tongue, men jump into their boats and shroud themselves in the comfort of warmth as they scamper for the thwarts and oars of their beloved; they do this with such urgency it is as though the entire town is on fire and they are the only firemen for miles around.

Not only were they in competition with others of similar mind, like Glover and Boyd, but were also in a timely chase against the second hand of a clock, for every breath was a milestone and a humpback could quite often break free of his capture, heading out to sea with the killers in tow. A lost whale was lost pay.

These men were not on a contract, were not promised good wages for the nil-return of blubber, but were only paid with what the headsman could suckle from the sellers of his merchandise. In most cases this was quite substantial, even though prices rose and fell like the waves of the sea, but mostly rewarding for the work conducted. Such business did provide good wages and on a regular basis, but when times were hard and money scarce the opportunity to pay on time was not always possible. Even so the men would not abandon their captain, and besides, the wages he paid the islanders, whites, half-castes and full-blooded aborigines, was the same all round: there was no racism here.

And so the men sit at table, playing cards and hunched over a cup of tea when all of a sudden the call comes from aloft a horse, the beast breathing heavy and being ridden like a champ, sprinting down towards where the men are housed....

RUSHO! RUSHO!

The men jumped to action as though nothing else mattered – and at that moment, nothing did. The killers now made a showing as cobbles were shook loose from the ground below the feet of men as they thundered down to the boats, the fresh morning air doused with the mist of action. Individuals clambered aboard their boat with quickened ease, oars picked up and thrust into position, the water of the bay quickly stroked in order to propel them ever forward and towards the prize which at this stage remained unclear. And then the spouting caught the eye of George, most definitely a humpback— no, two... two great beasts of the sea being forced into the bay by the hound dogs of the sea; the wolves of the water, the encumbrance of the baleen, and devils of the murky surrounds. They were the evil at the backs of angels, the shackles of torment, and above all, the dorsal of death.

Corralled now the two humpbacks were forced towards the boats that sped towards the battle of wills and the will of man is as strong, if not stronger, than a killer whale, for man would will himself to death in order to feed his family, where a killer whale would only stress itself to the limits of its energy, and where a battle is not won in good time and all strength is wasted away, the killers will fall back to try their luck on something more easily won.

Harpoons and lances were struck and stuck, the two whales secured within an hour of fighting, two boats with their sidekicks against two humpbacks of medium size. They were both good kills, secured within good time, and the relief that fell form the men's faces was apparent to even a blind man for their purses now had something to look forward to, even if for only a short time; about a thousand quids worth.

The drought had been watered, the show was on the road, and everyone thought how lucky they were with the good fortune of two such quick kills. And without second thought the humpbacks were anchored and buoyed, the killers taking their reward as they always did and the men made for shore. They would return on the morrow to bring home the bacon, but something was brewing, something further out and unfortunate, for the reason that the humpbacks had made for the coast and so easily captured was that they wished to avoid the storm fast approaching from the southeast.

That night the winds blew, the men's slumber being shaken from them like a strong wind wakes the deeply embedded roots of a gigantic tree. For three days the weather grew against in ferocity against them and their fears grew. The gases within the whales would have had their way with the carcasses after the first day, each floating to the surface, ready for harvest, but no move could be made upon them in this weather. The water around Whale Spit Beach was like a kettle on the boil, far too dangerous for little boats and men so fragile. It was a wonder in itself how such fortitude in men and their tools could be so easily swayed by the power of the sea, but that's the way it was, and will always be.

But on the fourth day it could be accepted no more and the boats forced themselves into the ferocity of the sea, the coast scoured both up and down for any sign of the whales they had left just four days before. They had broken from the anchors, were lost to the sea, would more than likely be afloat somewhere, but so far unattainable. Worst of all were the faces of the men. They had gone without wages for so long now. The thought that the drought at the commencement of the season was over, was optimistic to say the least. It was now that they had to be faced with the reality of the situation.

George walked in on the men as they sat in their gloom around the table of the kitchen, drinking tea and pondering on their next call to action. The headsman posed the trouble to them all, posted them well with the few choices open to them. But the men refused to hear of it, refused to admit defeat and rallied to their captain's side, to remain loyal. They would stay on and continue, sure in their minds that their fate was not written and that the tide would change soon enough, that the opportunity to deblubber more whales would be just around the corner. And it was indeed just like that for they had caught themselves two whales just a few days later and there was more to follow that, all told there was nine in as few as three weeks: their wages had been secured.

CHAPTER FIFTEEN

The conditioning of both species had sprung to life more than simple feelings, gestures, smiles and jumps for joy. There was camaraderie amongst them, for they each served the other, although from the killers point of view the humans were nothing more than pawns for which should be used to the best of their ability. But the understanding was there also and all the killers knew well that the duties performed by both parties amalgamated to cooperation.

They weren't competing for food but were in fact escalating their abilities by relying upon the energy and prowess of the other species. But there was always room for improvement, and yes, room for amazement.

The simple fact that both man and killer were working together was amazing enough but to the men of the boats it was all part of the day and working roll; the killers too, thought nothing more of the collaboration being anything other than manipulation tethered to a secular importance... the harvesting of their sustenance.

People and animals do all they can to secure a living, whether one receives money as reward or a meal for its effort, it is all one and the same. It is therefore of utmost importance to seek any opportunity which will reap the bigger harvest and in the shortest amount of time. This was something that Tom knew well and had put into practice many times in the past, but the time had arrived for a new weapon to be brought into view.

The flop-tailing had called the boats to duty as any other night. One boat was faster than the other which was a disappointment to the killers within the bay, for the more boats availed them meant a quicker kill and increased energy savings.

George's crew flashed ahead of Alex Grieg's boat, both separated by poor vision and a good football field of misery. But where the misery was a little longer suffered by Alex, it was short lived for George, for a right whale showed itself by spouting high and wide, moon beams glistening off the skin of the monster as it surfaces amongst the bubbling of the waters around it, the killers, every one, biting at the fish with all their might and thrashing about in the sea.

Arthur Ashby took his position with pride and hurled his harpoon with all the power he could muster. It stuck; the fast fish was secure. It then turned tail and commenced to head back out to sea, away from the two boats now behind it.

With the whale secured and the rope let out, the whale was in a prime position to pull George and his crew further away from shore then they would have liked; not only this but there was the other importance factor that Alex Grieg and his crew were falling further behind as they spurred themselves on by the power of the oars alone.

Tom saw the dilemma and acted immediately, pulling away from the fray and returning to George. The others of the small contingent looked upon him briefly and with anxiousness, opening their mouths, exposing their teeth, and noisily clapping their jaw together, voicing their anger and frustration at Tom's misdemeanour in vacating his post at such a time, but no sooner had they showed their displeasure in him and they realised that this is what Tom did, this is what he was about, and nothing could be done to change him.

With sudden amazement, Tom grabbed onto the whale line with sheer exuberance and allowed himself to be pulled alone by the whale, the green boat just a few metres behind him.

The men were flabbergasted to say the least and it took several moments for them to realise what was happening.

The very implication that Tom was helping the situation was sheer ludicrous; but there it was; ludicrous to one but common sense to another, and although brain size is no indication of intelligence, in this particular situation it appeared that it did.

Tom was in fact slowing the progress of the whale to such a degree that Alex Grieg and his crew were gaining ground upon the fight and gaining ground rather quickly.

With Tom in the way, George could not manoeuvre, but if Tom were not there then the crew would not be able to advance quick enough. It called upon them all to see the picture painted clear as can be: the other crew were catching up and were soon in a position where the harpooner of the other boat was standing with his leg within the concave of the thwart and letting loose with a second harpoon. Tom released his hold upon the line and joined the others of the pod.

A lance suddenly pierced the space between the ribs and the death-throws of the animal paved the way for the killer's show of exuberance. They festered in and tried to force their way into the mouth of the whale as blood flooded from the blowhole, tearing at the flesh of his lips and holding on for all the glory to follow.

The whale was putting up a hell of a fight and at one stage leapt more than five metres out of the sea with three killers still attached to his lips, a sight never to be forgotten by the men of the green boat as they looked up open-mouthed from the thwarts where their backsides remained glued.

The right whale was leasing his energy for no reward and within another five minutes the fight was over; the combined efforts of man and beast had won over another mammal of the sea.

With the whale marked in the usual, both anchor and markers attached, a second task dawned upon George as was always the case for someone so readily on their toes and willing to work. He looked over the men to give his orders as the killers grabbed the whale and took her deep, into the murky waters of the sea, out of sight and out of mind. They would do as they pleased with the whale and within 24 hours should be afloat and ready to be towed. But to the moment all reflected.

They had secured a kill just the other day and the whale was not far from where they were; just a few kilometres in fact. Instead of waiting for the morrow he decided that the opportunity should not be passed up and the two crews were handed the task of bringing the bacon home to fry.

It didn't take them long to find the animal as the gases had floated it as usual and on time; the only thing left now was to tow the beast back to the try-works which was some seven kilometres away. The night was pleasant though cold, the moon shone out in good quantity and it seemed that the task ahead was achievable.

The markers were pulled in and the anchor too, several ropes attached to the carcass and the men braced for the hard slog home. Their backs broke under the strain, for seven kilometres was a big ask. The tide seemed to be a little against them and to the moon George looked in wonder, high up and behind him. With time the satellite would makes its way across the sky and to the west where it was hoped that relief would soon follow in the form of a little tide, but that was so far away that they could only think of the hot feed that would be awaiting them on their return, a return to the bunkhouse which could be just hours away.

Although the weather seemed to be in their favour the work they had achieved prior to attempting the long haul had drained them of all the energy they had. There were no super heroes amongst them, just flesh and bone which was commanded over by brains and brawn, and a discipline that comes by way of the strongest motivation.

They pulled upon the oars with all their strength, continued on as best they could against the tide. The lights ahead of them showed where Twofold Bay lay but it was very far away.

After several hours of pulling the floating monster behind them they appeared to be making very little progress, their hardened hands starting to show signs of over-work and strain. Another thirty minutes and George waved the white flag... they would head on home without the cargo and return in the morning; after a good night's rest... or what remained of it.

CHAPTER SIXTEEN

It was in 1904 that the number of killer whales within the pod was to be altered by one and such an unfortunate event it was.

George held the power of the rudder in his palms and steered pleasurably out towards the mouth of the bay where a whale was buoyed and expected to have come to the surface already; all that was needed now was for the beast to be towed to the try-works where the deblubbering could commence in earnest, where the men would surrender themselves to the back-breaking work, suffering the intolerable smell and flies, the seagulls afloat the breeze pestering for whatever they could get their greedy beaks upon.

One of the men in the boat was suddenly drawn to a chase and pointed it out to the others. It appeared that Jackson was chasing a grampus, gaining ground on the dolphin which sped through the surf in an all inspiring effort to escape its devastating future; the bleak and unconditional devouring which was to fall upon it.

The men smiled as they watched chase and pulled upon their oars when fright suddenly fell upon them, an anxiousness that lasted for but mere seconds as they continued to look upon the scene so far away.

Jackson had propelled himself so well through the shallow waters that washed themselves upon the beach that as the chase was about to meet its end the grampus moved aside and Jackson fell upon the sandy beach; high and dry, only the bottom portion of his body feeling the comfort of the sea upon him.

He thrashed about in an effort to free himself from the predicament as the grampus made its way safely beck towards the open sea and the men could see the dilemma that Jackson was in. He was too far from the water's edge to secure delivery back into his watery surrounds without the assistance of the men within the green boat. Without further ado they steered towards the killer as he continued to flap about and try with all his might to gain ground upon the retreating waves, the moon high in the sky, upon the other side of the world, pulling the tide out as it does on its journey around the earth.

The men felt that they had little time to procure a rescue, for the killer would not function well upon the beach of Twofold Bay, and even as they rowed several gulls saw this as an opportunity to flap on down and stand their ground out of harm's way, looking upon the giant killer with eyes as large as saucers, squawking as their stomachs ached to be filled, wishing with all their will to be able to peck out the eyes and given the smallest opportunity to savour what they could of this offering to them. It was then that a figure came into view, walking along the beach and towards the killer, every step deliberate and full. It was Harry Silks, homeless and obtuse; he'd seen Jackson washed ashore upon Aslings Beach; quite by accident.

The men collaborated on the man as he suddenly sprang into action, seeing the George and his green boat filled with men. Silks commenced to run rather rapidly towards Jackson. He wished to be first upon the scene; but why?

The men continued upon their salvation of the killer that meant so much to them for they knew too well that Silks would not be able to move the monstrous body and blubber that was Jackson back into the surf that ebbed in and out, the white of the curling waves disappearing as they rolled upon the stretch of sand.

And that was when the horror of the situation shook them to their very foundations, where it become impossible to fathom the outcome which was about to unfold. Instead of giving aid to the whale, and in full view of a Davidson crew, Silks did withdraw a knife from a scabbard and stabbed the defenceless whale to death, followed quite quickly by his running away from the building insults and threats that were flung his way.

Several of the other killers were drawn to the sounds of the splashing flukes, where Jackson's tail was able to affect sufficient disturbance upon the water that others would rally to the scene. They too were struck hard with the horrific scene and perceived it as it should be perceived... wanton slaughter. It was then that Tom and the other killers departed the bay for a few days, simply shocked and exasperated, depressed and shattered.

What would become of the contract between man and beast? Unknown to the killer whales, Silks was escorted out of town by the local law enforcers for his own protection, never to be seen of again.

A stand had to be made and Fearless Davidson undertook to repair the damage done and began legal action to have the killers protected by law by first writing a letter to the Eden Progress

Association, and although the killers themselves would not know of his efforts, he himself would feel as though some form of justice had been served.

Within a few days another humpback was corralled by the killers, although there appeared to be fewer of them than before. The night was dark and peaceful and the whale was relatively easy to catch. It easily drew the men's attention to see that the killers still provided them with aid but the full devastating effect of Jackson's killing would show its face soon enough, where the pod size would be drastically reduced, fewer and fewer of their dogs would return to receive aid from the men in the capture of their lip and tongue.

CHAPTER SEVENTEEN

Stranger was dead, killed by a fisherman in Botany Bay, August 1907. She was mother to Tom and Hooky, and quite expectedly these two killers of the sea, so fond of Twofold Bay, felt the power of the separation bite them harder than anything else they had experienced in their entire life. It wasn't just the matter of fact that their mother had died, nor that the matriarch of their community was existed no longer; but it was the horror of human intervention that troubled them most. Their mother had been killed by a fisherman for no other reason than to spite the species for taking away with the fish that he looked upon as being provided him for his net. Of all the killer whales in the world, not a single one had ever been know, by man, to have killed a man; but of all the men in the world, plenty had knowingly killed a killer.

What was it that drove a killer whale 'not' to take the life of a man? Was it the killer's sense that a human was intelligent? Why should intelligence procure sanctity and life? The killer whale, without religion or innovation, had proved to be more human than man himself.

It is not surprising, therefore, to notice that both Tom and Hooky were vacant the bay that year, to return afresh on the following, bringing with them a new invigoration and determination.

Cooper and Big Ben on the other hand, more than just friends of Stranger, found the parting to be too much to bear. They departed the pod of Twofold Bay almost immediately with Young Ben their son. Albert, their daughter, chose to remain behind, having mothered Charlie Adgery in the spring of 1900. Shortly after further demise struck the pod for news soon arrived that Big Ben was dead, dying when stranded on the rocks at Leatherjacket Bay, and within a few months Young Ben returned without his father, to regain a little of what solace he could.

It was a terrible year for the pod of killers, affecting them all in some small or large way. First there was Jackson in 1904, and now Stranger, followed shortly after by Big Ben.

Times were changing; the vibrations and smells within the sea told them that. They were growing old and their minds were weary, full of good memories slowly evaporating to be replaced by bad.

What was to become of it all?

CHAPTER EIGHTEEN

Whaling was whaling. To the men of Twofold Bay it mattered little – other than the price they were to receive for the catch for the amount of effort and time displaced – whether the whale caught was big or small. Equipment was important, the boats being the most blessed of all they possessed. If a reasonable catch could be secured for as little outlay as possible and with no damage dealt upon the boats then it was a good catch and one worth remembering. But one of the most remembered will be little reflected upon by history books, even though a record of the grandest proportion – which will never be broken for bay whaling is no longer practised – and that was the capture of the thirty metre long blue whale of 1910.

The sheer size made the catch a momentous occasion for those at the oars but it wasn't so much a case of capture than surrender.

The blue whale had a calf with her that measured a little over half the mother's length, a mother of a whale which totalled 98 tonnes, enough oil and bone to tear the stitches of any money bag, regardless of form and manufacture.

The call of RUSHO! went out firm and loud as it had at any other time in the past, the panting of the horse from the lookout being accompanied by the flop-tailing of Tom at the Kiah. Boats were manned and the waters entered in readiness to secure another humpback, but what they met made them stare in disbelief.

By the time they positioned themselves in readiness to deliver their prowess, George sitting with shoulders back and ready to deliver all hell upon the blue whale, the killers had hounded the mother to such desperate levels that she breached herself upon the shore and became easy pickings; the killers had carried their task out so well that the blue whale was out of reach of them and they missed their lip and tongue, but they had their way with the calf. It was the least exciting of all the catches they could remember but one of the most satisfying.

The band of just six killers had done their job well, a small number in comparison to those that were currently not so far away and further up the coast, a task which would have taken longer to perform is further out to sea. Without the aid of the jagged shore the killers alone could not have achieved victory over the blue whale and could easily have lost her. The sheer exuberance that the member of Hooky's pod felt surging through them was too much to express without the show-boating of their jumping from the sea and crashing back again upon its surface.

It was a trophy to be remembered amongst the old saddle patches and the new, Kinscher and Little Jack, daughter and son of Big Jack herself, showing once and for all that skill was a lesson taught and handed down, not just a gift of chance. But what of Tom; what made him so different? What was it that drove his ambition and aptitude? What was it that founded his strong, unequivocal and unbreakable sufferance? Why did he display a heavenly allegiance to man?

Tom was a pioneer, and one and only, a creature bound by the fruits of intelligence which left the others of his species far behind in understanding. He understood, he was a freak of nature, like the 'Ghosts of the Darkness', the lions of Africa that devoured man through superior intellect and cunning, he too had unequalled knowledge and instincts of deliberation. Tom was a powerhouse of ability and procurement, a wealth of interpretation within his head busting at the seams to escape his shell and yell out to the world that he was there to pave the way to the bright light of bonding, a bonding that even Darwin, a man of generous, failed to see in full bloom.

Tom was similar to mortal man; he could feel hurt and embarrassment, fear death and display great courage, but above all, Tom had the ability to see beyond the makeup pasted upon a man's exterior as an astronomer sees beyond the makeup of the universe.

CHAPTER NINETEEN

Jimmy fought well on this day, the day of his birth some 31 years before.

He'd arrived at Twofold Bay several years after the death of Typee. It was a time of upheaval when some killers departed and others strayed in, at a time the pod was still large and prosperous but had to deal with minor issues of command and structure; though little did it matter under the sway of Stranger in the years past, who for her years and with the power bestowed, stood as a strong matriarch with a long list of signals and attack manoeuvres accredited to her name.

Jimmy was quite normally a quiet mammal and far less boisterous than those like Tom. He was mated with Big Jack, a female of a line outside of that known within the pod, both her mother and father being 'offshore' variants more apt to live off fish, particularly salmon, than anything else. Tired of their life and position in the pod of 70-odd other killers they had opted for a life of habitual change and so found their way to Twofold Bay where they stayed for several years before moving on. Jimmy, having founded a life for himself, and a mate in Big Jack, stayed on.

Big Jack had mothered two killers within the Eden pod and they were Kinscher and Little Jack, respectively a female and a male.

Over the past twelve months, Jimmy's persona in the pod of 15 had grown quite substantially, though not because of any great feats noteworthy of praise, but because Big Jack had been recognised as matriarch since 1907. Jimmy felt more than honoured to be in the position he was in and the very idea of his being some sort of representative brought on a blossom of change in regards to effort and effect, though only to small degree. Such an effort was accepted well by the other members of the pod for they understood well the situation he was in.

So there came a day when a humpback had been cornered once again and the familiar assaults upon the floating casket of blubber continued as they had in the past, with much effort being placed upon trying to tire the beast out and to create as much stress and horror for the humpback as was possible.

Again and again the blowhole was covered, killer after killer throwing themselves upon the back of the whale in order to impede its breathing, helping prevent the whale from sounding and turning to the open gate of Twofold Bay for an eventual escape.

The men too, were present upon the surface of the sea, prodding away with their sticks of iron, shifting their position with oars and yelling out above the noise of war to try and bring the whale to a standstill.

Several harpoons had been thrown this day and one was not well secured, though the second had done its job well and lancing had begun as usual. The whale was putting up a good fight until a last ditch effort by Jimmy saw him move in for the kill, to suffocate the whale and then rip at its flank to create further injury and insult to the humpback.

And then something went horribly wrong. With so many lines in the water and so much confusion floating about the scene of battle, Jimmy become entwined within the line and sank with the humpback. The other killers simply assisted the humpback to the bottom of the bay, initially unaware of Jimmy's predicament, and the effects of the battle upon the men was so great that they too failed to see anything amiss.

Kinscher and Little Jack were quickly alerted to the situation when Jimmy was heard crying out, unable to break free of the cumbersome mess that he had fatally attracted to himself. There was little they could do, however, and Jimmy died there within the bay he'd come to love so much, in the comfort of the love and company of Kinscher, Little Jack, Big Jack and the other members of the pod.

And so several of the pod fell to the pressures of the loss. Big Jack soon departed as she could deal with the situation no more, Walker (son of Humpy) following in her wake. Young Ben, having returned for two years after the death of his mother now departed for good, the loss of his friend weighing too much upon his mind – there had been too much death in the past. Last but not least the following turned their flukes upon the bay and left for deeper waters; Albert, Skinner and Little Jack.

The following day the carcass was retrieved by George and his crew, utterly astounded at what they found when they drew nearer the scene of the floating carcass, buoyed and anchored where they had left the humpback. Jimmy was strapped to its side as though belonging, like a baby strapped to its mother. Such a scene had never been seen before and it jolted the crew as they looked on, cutting the line away and allowing Jimmy to float away from view. They were reminded of the time Humpy had fouled the lines but she was more fortunate for the predicament was noticed prior to the whale sinking, Humpy cut from the lines and set free before death had the chance to pull the final curtain closed.

The men remembered this day as the tragedy it was, as too did the killer whales out to sea. The whalers cut a remembrance into the woodwork of Boyd's Tower, Jimmy to be remembered forever along with Peter Lia.

CHAPTER TWENTY

The Norwegians had mustered 9,500 barrels of oil from the east coast of Australia in 1913, the last for them, and they lay up their three chasers; but this was a small tally when compared to other companies of the same game. But the damage was done and the killer whale was vacant from the waters of Twofold Bay for great stints of time, but a familiar fin was seen once more as it glided through the gentle waves near the Kiah Inlet and this was accompanied by smiles upon the faces of those who knew him best. Tom was back with Humpy, Hooky, Sharkey, Brierly, Youngster, Kinscher and Charlie Adgery.

It was at these times that the cooperation between beast and man continued as in the past, with much reflection upon old times falling upon them all. Reflections of securing a 'fast fish', reflections upon the unwritten laws between the two species, and reflections upon the feeding upon lips and tongues of those slaughtered so that the killers could survive and the men upon the shore could receive the opportunity to make their blessed money.

Other killers came and went over the years, although few in number, and whales were killed as they had always been, with great cooperation and effort on the part of both man and killer of the sea. It was by no surprise that Tom and George forgot how it had been before their time when the laws were a blossoming flower, each law opening up a new beginning; but the end was near and the killers so few.

One of the more horrid of circumstances to hit the pod of killers was the death of Sharkey (Jackson's partner), who in a clash with the Norwegians was slaughtered due to her attempts to feed upon the offerings of the sea. The Norwegians saw the killers as a pest more than anything else and so Sharkey bought the brunt of their anger. Brierly and Youngster then chose to depart the bay of horrors for eternity.

There was no bitterness in this, the fact that all were growing old and becoming just a little less reliant than in past years, but they noticed little for the whaling industry was faltering at the head as the killer's number diminished.

And as the years progressed fewer and fewer killers returned to the slaughter grounds.

CHAPTER TWENTY-ONE

World War II was soon upon them and men disappeared from the boats to do their duty overseas. By the time the war was over only a handful of killers ever showed up at the onset of the whaling season, where winter broke upon the bay and its inhabitants, and the boats were more often than not manned by casuals rather than men of iron and full of character.

Spring came and went and then summer, autumn and winter as usual, the same game played year in and year out. On the odd occasion there were only three killers, at others there would be five, but the aggressiveness of the killer whales always remained heightened, even though individuals slowed a little in their old age; all that was except Tom who was as young as he'd ever been. And as the pod decreased in size George's own family grew and the years fell behind them all, Kinscher and Charlie Adgery leaving the pod in 1923.

And George too, in all comparison with his colleagues of the sea, was as fearless as he had always been; they were peas in a pod, one and the same, a strong bond having been struck between the two.

Never before in the history of man, save the rumours of a man in the jungles of some far away country living with wolves, had man and beast performed so well together, a performance you would swear had been orchestrated well; but it was familiarity and trust that made them unique.

In the early twenties, Tom would quite often be seen to grab hold of the painter (anchor rope), it having been thrown to him, and he would grasp it and tow the boat towards a whale, more often than not several killers aiding in the antic that saw a fast approach made upon an angry whale of enormous size, speedily overtaking any opposition that might be otherwise trying to get to the whale before the Davidsons, holding dearly onto the 60 fathoms of 2 inch coir rope. Tom did this in order to secure the kill, for he needed the sustenance in order to survive. Without the aid of George, Tom would meet his end all the sooner.

Eden Fisherman, Jackie Warren, even witnessed the phenomena known as Tom in 1926, where he purposely grabbed the anchor line beneath Jack Davison's boat and towed him along the surface of the sea, not for the purpose of chasing down a humpback, but for the fun of it, and Margaret Brooks having her breathe taken away by the whales antics as Tom pulled against her father's boat the 'White Heather', tugging hard on the tow rope, trying heaven and earth to prevent him from towing a dead whale into the bay, depriving the killers of the 'Law of the Tongue'.

Yes indeed, they were times to remember, times that saw little evaluation in the annals of history.

Soon, however, there was only Tom and two others. Most of the others had taken to different waters to secure meals of similar and different variety, neither joining super pods nor really deviating from them, but remaining unto themselves. Several of the pod broke away and commenced their own of matrilineal linkage, and some died as whales do. It seemed to Tom that his entire life had been spent with the men of Twofold Bay and it was to him a family bond of its own. They had come to rely on one another as species do in times of hardship, where bonding takes many years, if not decades, to meld into one. As for Tom's family; well, he had little to show for his merits as a male for his offspring had separated from him when their mother refused to leave her pod of transients; but he was never alone.

Year after year saw fewer whales secured and the killers were forced to pursue other means of nourishment and from other hunting grounds that had proved fruitful to their needs, to the great disappointment of old friends.

CHAPTER TWENTY-TWO

So many years behind him and so many deaths. George could only be thankful that his experiences to date were vastly good and with few of horror. But old memories die and new ones fill the void, in particular where devastation is the result.

George had a son by the name of Jack, and he in turn was married with three children... this is the recollection of how Tom gave a little dignity back to his friend, George in 1926:

There came a day where the small family of five, along with several other relatives, met with a horrific accident near the Kiah River and their dinghy was submerged in the freakish weather, just metres from home. Dozens of family and friends delivered themselves to the search over the coming days where two little ones – Roy and Patrician – were missing along with Jack Davidson.

It was a sad fact of fate that saw three deaths in one day, in a storm which lashed out its evil in more than one way. The fact of the case is as basic as one, two, three. Tom was not far from the bay but remained near Leatherjacket, more for comfort than anything else; had he been nearer to the call for aid then he would have availed himself immediately to the care of those in need. This he proved over the coming days by entering Twofold Bay and approaching the scene where many boats searched frantically for the bodies of the three that were missing.

The two children were found soon enough; the girl pulled deceased from shallow water and the boy's body from the sandy bottom, only his legs visible. As for Jack, nothing could be found.

Tom could see that something was amiss but didn't understand what. The men were searching for something, going over the sea floor time and time again with their boats and grappling hooks, looking for signs of something they had lost.

Tom then bombarded the area with the skills taken for granted, the signals received by his senses forming the picture clear within his mind. He could see the body of Jack beneath the surface, under the sand where the boats had searched to no avail. For the next few days after the tragedy, the weather became beautiful and serine, Tom continued up and down in front of the bar, trying with all his presence to show the world what he knew; that he had found the remains of the one they were searching.

George looked upon his friend of the sea with great admiration, seeing Tom's presence, in this time of need, as a mark of great respect, and it suddenly dawned upon him that Tom might just be trying to tell him something. But how could that be, for the area was searched over and over, not a trace of Jack to be found.

Tom could see the expression upon George's face, the sparkle of wonder in his eyes, the methodical ticking away of the brain with his head, a brain of no comparison to his own. Tom could see without doubt that George had stumbled upon the antics of his demeanour and called for the boat to do another sweep, to search the area where Tom had indicated by his persistence, and before the hour was out they found Jack's body beneath the sand of the inlet and drew him upon the shore; Tom followed the boat in, paying his respects.

The other two had been buried just two days before Jack and now it was his turn, more than 40 cars full of those wishing to pay their respects following the hearse as it drew into the cemetery opposite the bay and in spy-hopping view of Tom as he contemplated the ceremony. Never before had he seen such a large congregation of men together in one spot, at one time and in complete silence, only the soft tones of the priest lifting themselves to the wind and floating down to be heard by the single killer in the bay.

Tom had completed his task and completed it well, and offered assistance to his friend which was beyond the call of duty. Tom owed this man nothing but still felt the bond as strongly as George. The bond could never be broken. To Tom, George was his family, the only family he's ever really needed. Without the bond between them both it was doubtful that Tom would have lived as long as his did.

The men had served him well, as he served them, but to Tom it was a one-way ticket of servitude for the taste of lip and tongue, the very sustenance that it offered, was beyond all compare: what did he care what they did with a humpback's body after its death; it meant little to him? But the service he had paid this man of men was not forgotten, could never be forgotten, and on the conclusion of the service, George did pay a visit to the shore; not to pay his respects to jack by laying visit upon his place of death but to say a heart-felt thankyou to his true friend of the sea.

It was then that Tom turned into the bay and made way for the remainder of his pod, a humpback whale and her calf allowing themselves to be caught unawares. The fight was on and the other two members of the pod were anxious for help.

He turned and thrust his flukes, speeding through the water, slicing through the waters of the bay, and to the waiting struggle which simply had to be won, for they had been without food for quite some time, and as George had lost Jack to the ever waking sea, Tom too, lost a friend this year, for Hooky, son of Stranger, fathered by a stray, a great pod leader and easily recognised by his dorsal fin and the way in which it was bent at 45 degrees, left Twofold Bay for all time. It was time to face the facts as they were played before them. The crew was made up of mostly new faces; they seemed inexperienced and inept when compared to the likes of those in years past, at a time before the war took the men away in droves.

The crew was one boat manned by faces that were ever changing; the sea was giving up less and less opportunities to make a kill; above all, they were growing old and weary and the times called for a substitute, a morsel of food which would be easier to quarry; less palatable but just as rewarding when considering the overall effect that a full stomach of food had on a killer whale.

And so the face of the industry, for those of Twofold Bay, was drawing to a close.

CHAPTER TWENTY-THREE

And then there was only Humpy and Tom, frolicking in the bay as they had done when they were young. But there was a difference of course; they weren't as agile as they once were and so they projected themselves out of the water with less... ambition. A stranger passing by upon the shore might look down upon them both and think how free-spirited they were; playing as though without a trouble in the world, young and looking for mischief; but to George... he knew the truth, understood it all. The killer whales were old, growing short in the tooth, age beginning to portray them all.

1927 and the pod of two seemed not to have a care in the world. Once a pod of over fifty, strong in every virtue, a great repertoire of song and voice allowing them to corral humpbacks and other whales with great ease, permitting them to push the whale towards the men and their boats, to secure a meal all the sooner.

Humpy: older than Tom and even frailer. She was partnered with Typee and gave birth to Jackson, had heard of her son's death at the hands of Silks and his demented mind but did not understand all, for killer whales do not convey ideas like men and their patterned speech. She had once led attack after attack upon whales, had ripped chunks from their lips and flank, and even once become entangled most temporarily in the line attached to a whale and then freed by George. She led a pod until 1980 and on her return in 1885 became next in line for position as matriarch after Big Jack, and mother of Walker who had left the pod after the death of Jimmy.

Yes indeed, there was a great history here, a story to be told, a silent story which resided in the memories of Tom and Humpy. But Humpy's days were almost over.

They had both heard a humpback some miles out to sea and had followed in her wake for some time before deciding on a move against it. It was a move without the aid of man, one that they would regret. It was the same as any other, the attack launched in the normal manner... nothing different, apart from their number.

They took chunk after chunk from the whale, pressed home the stress and fear, overwhelming the whale with bitter-sweet aggression, for aggression was a double-edged sword; it acted for the killers by hurrying up the cause of death, and it heightened the aggressive nature of the whale as it endeavoured to succeed in an escape or to bring about its conclusion by causing injury to one or more of its attackers.

And so it is here, far out to sea, that Humpy received a wound to the face, an eye lost in the fight; she was now deprived of her abilities as a hunter.

The whale made its escape as Tom came in close to his friend of the sea; a friend no-closer could he have been. They had succeeded in having a good fill on the blubber of the whale but this would not last them long. The line had now been drawn for

Humpy. Within the week she was dead and Tom was left to compete for food on his own. No longer would he be able, nor willing, to attempt an attack upon a humpback... unless it was a calf.

CHAPTER TWENTY-FOUR

And so now there was just Tom; he died on 16th September 1930, just before midnight, the 17th unveiling the end of a legend in his own right.

A week before his death he had put chase to a grampus, taking chunks from the mammal of the sea until it died. It was a fairly quick death and short fight, though took a lot out of Old Tom. His teeth bared the brunt of his years, being specifically worn down in areas where he had taken the painter in his jaws, where his efforts to assist the men upon their boats had proved a devastating blow against George's opposition.

The grampus was a meal not to be forgotten, a great treat for an old warhorse, the blubber, lips and tongue taken great advantage of, a feeding fit for a king. And the spectacle drew a little crowd for it dawned upon all those of Twofold Bay that Old Tom was alone, not another killer to be seen.

Tom had remained loyal to the end, a friend of those he had come to know, and more people knew of him than he could possibly know of them. But that is where the killer whale dies and the legend lives on, for it was a week later that he was found dead after a day of frolicking in the bay, flop-tailing into the breeze as the setting sun said it's good night.

Yes indeed, he enjoyed those last hours, showing himself most temporarily upon the surface, inside the bay, onlookers seeing for themselves that something was amiss; the next day his body floated into Snug Cove in Twofold Bay, recognised without mistake by his tall and distinctive dorsal fin which had been photographed so many times in the past and even caught on camera in 1910. He died, simply, from old age in the accompaniment of starvation.

It was now, as his body lay still upon the beach that his genitalia proved once and for all that he was in fact a male, but how had he managed to live for so long is beyond anyone to understand... somewhere between 60 and 80 years by all comparison to realistic witness reports [as we cannot prove his date of birth].

J.R.Logan suggested that preservation was the key in order for Tom's story to remain alive and well and for such a suggestion saw to it that his skeleton was provided a home in a purpose built museum, funded for by Logan, himself.

The Eden Killer Whale Museum still exists today and puts the minds of all those that visit into a spin over the tales that can be told or simply uncovered. No one can deny the truth, for the truth is documented so well.

Tom was a male orca, 6.7 metres long and with a dorsal fin of 1.7 metres high. He was fairly short when compared to other Orcas in other seas, but there were different casts of killer as there were races of people.

CHAPTER TWENTY-FIVE

Tom was gone and bay whaling had come to an end. George Davidson hung up his harpoon and lances in 1932, the crew disbanding to find other ways in which to support themselves and their families, but a majority of the crew were nothing more them helpers, there to assist, like the sergeant of the local police station.

Other orcas that were known to the bay whalers came back from time to time, laying visit upon the mouth of the Kiah River, but these visits saw little action being taken out against a humpback, for the tide was changing and whaling right across the country was dying fast.

It is strange to understand, from the human point of view, how killer whales could change their tactics of the hunt so proficiently after almost 90 years of going through the same routines, chasing whales off the coast, helping themselves to tongue and lip. But they were adverse and could turn miracles of nature when required, and the pod simply relocated to other feeding grounds, understanding full well that their easy feeding was over and that they now had to make the next best choice in where to get their meals from.

But even now as the darkness continues to fall over George and the life of the pods during the 90 years of their presence (not considering the interaction with the Yuin), where bay whaling existed for one hundred, that killer whales continue to return to Eden, and they are the descendants of the pods that once roamed these waters, for it is hard to change ones destiny when imbedded in a 90 year old tradition. And the humpback whales frequent the bay and splash around playfully, their calves by the sides enjoy the warmth of the water, feeding without a concern for being attacked; and George watched from the sidelines.

And even today, in 2008 and beyond, from the darkness of time comes a reminder of the past, for even now killer whales can be seen sporting in the waters near Twofold Bay, where the picturesque port town and its ocean views, and forest surrounds, continue to relax all that see it, providing great delight to those that lay visit.

And here right now it is an honour to declare that science is on the killer's side, for they can confirm, quite adamantly, that they are intelligent creatures with astonishing acoustic senses, social coordination, and self-awareness. They are able to learn rapidly, are innovative and can manipulate objects. They freely interact with human beings and are a delight to work with.

CHAPTER TWENTY-SIX

To an Orca the human race is little more than a hindrance, in particular where excessive amounts of commercial blubber has continued to be exploited from the oceans and seas of the world. From right along the coasts of the countries of this world, to the pen seas and the areas around the Antarctic and Arctic, whales have been openly slaughtered for the oil that they contain. However, unbeknown to the killers of Eden the International Whaling Conference of 1945, held in London, prepared extensive regulations which would see to the part-protection of species of all whales. This was followed up in 1946 by a meeting in Washington by the International Whaling Commission which drew the conclusion that international regulations should be put into place and maintained.

The conservation of, not necessarily the whales themselves, but the stock levels, was somewhat agreed upon and passed so that from 1949 a solar gathering of members have come together and spoken on the maintaining of principle and projects which included the protection of species, in particular the females and their calves, sanctuaries and limitations on the number of animals to be killed in any 'open season'.

The depletion of whale numbers has since slowed but not altogether ceased. The blatant killing over the decades was one reason of many why killer whales tended to deviate from their feeding routes and normal routines but in the case of Twofold Bay the humans actually helped the killers gain food and didn't exploit them: if anything, the killer whale was exploiting man.

Twofold Bay offered much to the killers of Eden; not only was it a natural corral for which to entrap baleen but it was shallow enough to restrict a whale's escape. Leatherjacket Bay was also a natural wonder which was employed well by the killers for the currents during the season of whaling was most suited to their endeavours: the moderate current permitted the killers swim at a leisurely pace but maintain position in particular when it came time to sleep.

It was all a matter of strategy to the killer whale. They chose the ground upon where the killing was to take place and the method by which it was to be inflicted.

CHAPTER TWENTY-SEVEN

George Davidson was dead. It is 1952 and he dies with his memories intact. He was not alone in death, with loved ones so close and Tom inside his head. The relationship between the two will live on forever. It is a slice of history of which Australia should be proud; not so much for the establishment of the relationship between man of land and mammal of sea, but for the very acts of love and affection shared between the two species.

If we look deep enough we can see how the men under George Davidson gave up much to be able to work effectively with the killers of Twofold Bay. Their equipment was of the old school; their techniques were of the old school; their foresight was of the old school.

These were not greedy men and nor were they wicked or cruel. They had a job to do and did it well. They did believe, however, that they were manipulating the killer whale to meet their needs.

How is it that a killer whale can put behind it the nature of the sea; the nature of the species; the torments of their world? These killer whales befriended man and used him well to gain their food. They learnt to work with man and maintained a working relationship for many decades.

If all killer whales were the same then we could assume there would be more of this cooperation; but there is not. Instead we are drawn to the reality for the situation whereby one killer, and one killer only, took a situation and manifested it to suit the needs of matriarch and pod.

The name Tom should be celebrated for he was a one and only, possibly never again to be experienced by any of us living in this day and age.

Maybe the future will behold another just like him but for George and his memories, the last fragments of peace that drift from his mind on meeting with death, Tom was simply a friend who could never be forgotten. It is to Tom's testament that George has recorded some of his fondest memories.

HISTORY

Something that may well have helped influence the killer whale activity in Twofold Bay are the factors surrounding the hunting of the sperm whale.

1712 (Sperm Whale)

It was in 1712 that the first of the sperm whale was taken from the safe harbour of its home in the sea near Nantucket, far from the waters of the Australian coast, but where several ancestors of those in the Eden pod had once frequented. The oil was considered much more valuable than that harvested from the bay whalers, shore fishing which had been a development of the Red Indians in similarity, but not a perfect union as that of the Yuin of Twofold Bay. Deep sea whaling was now an investment anxiously pursued; the curtain had been raised and the slaughter begun; an infringement of the Orca's right to feed on all that swam in any of the seven seas.

1788 (Sperm Whale)

The settlement of Australia takes hold at the same time that the

South Pacific is exploited for what it holds within its parlour of delights, 1,800 souls shipped to Botany Bay as two great nations commence fishing within its waters.

1790s (Sperm Whale)

By the 1790s sperm whale fishing had spread to more favourable grounds, where they were seen to be in such large numbers that the opportunity could not be refused, hence the decimation of the South Pacific did commence, and although the killer whale tended to lay more towards the coastlines of many countries for their sustenance, routes across the great expanses of sea was patrolled.

1791 (Sperm Whale)

Many shoals were seen by members of the ship Britannia, from Van Diemen's Land to just out from the coast of Port Jackson, at approximately 15 kilometres, and the numerous sightings were recorded for the prosperity of the captain but divulged, in the end, to the governor for the Australian people and its fishing industry. The endeavours and efforts, therefore, of the human race helped dictate, within reasonable terms, that the killers should direct their attentions more favourably to the coastline where migratory routes of humpback were known to exist.

Within a few short years of this sighting another was recorded to the west of the Galapagos Islands where sperm whales were seen in large quantities, copulation a common occurrence. It was now a basis of knowledge, something known by the killers for centuries, that one particular migratory route lead along the coast of East Australia and out towards the islands so famous of

Darwin and his findings. Not only this but the waters of the Pacific, to the north-east of New Zealand, were bountiful with sperm whale and their off-spring, so much so that the vast area, too large to contemplate, was combed by ships of many nationalities including those from Australia.

1799

Matthew Flinders stood upon the deck and saw that Twofold Bay could easily make a grand harbour, the skeleton of a right whale visible on the beach. A thought then traversed his mind where he was reminded of the days of Captain Cook, where he very nearly entered the East coast of Australia at the point where Twofold Bay opened itself to the world, but due to bad weather was forced to the north where Botany Bay was chosen for the first settlement.

1804

It wasn't long before the commercial value of whaling hit the minds of those that continued to colonize Tasmania, where right whales (sometimes referred to as black whales) frequented the bays with their calves from June to October. This provided great opportunity to hunt sperm whale during the summer months and then the bay whales in winter, where, through the exuberance of those that lanced the whales till their hearts content, fell upon the realization that hunting from row boats was as good, if not better, than ramming home their harvest from large ships; bay whaling was now a true profession and taken up by a few bays along the coast of Australia where migratory whales tempted the greed and thirst of human desire for oil.

Sites were selected with great care as many considerations needed to take point, namely shelters for the men, cookhouse, cooperage (where casks and barrels of all description could be made and repaired, to be filled to the brim with that marvellous substance), storehouses and try-works where slabs of blubber could be easily drawn up a ramp and prepared for boiling, extracting the gold so laboriously sought.

1828

It soon became an interest, the Yuin and their exploits, and Twofold Bay made the headlines in a Sydney newspaper, bay whaling adopted soon after as more of an experiment than anything else. The spoils were so great that the opportunity could not be ignored. It was shortly after that 16 white men of a dispatch from Sydney were killed and another five years elapsed before Dr. A. Imlay secured over a thousand acres of land in the area.

The indigenous people of the region around Twofold Bay are called Yuin and had a name for the killers; they called them 'Beowas', meaning brothers or kin, they were 'transient, a social organization of killer whale which was set aside from the 'resident' and 'offfshore', but with many 'resident' characteristics; they were, in essence, a 'matrilineal' organisation of killers that were, to a degree, inseparable.

As per the Romans and Greeks before them, the Aboriginals of Australia looked upon the killer whales with great respect and admiration, believing wholeheartedly that they were the reincarnation of ancestors past, where the dead took the form of a wolf of the sea. Why?

The Yuin believed that the killer whales were the returned spirits of the dead, ancestors that had come back to the world of the living and to help provide sustenance to the indigenous population. If a monster of the deep was to provide such great amounts of food for the tribe then it must be nothing less than the re-incarnated spirit of a recently deceased member for their society. They were, every one, treasured as original members of the tribe and known, not only to help feed the Yuin, but also to protect them whilst in the water.

For long before the presence of any white man, the Yuin – not exploiting – made good advantage of the situation where it was quite common for baleen whales to be herded into the bay and become stranded upon the beach, whereby the strategies of the hunt become a symbolised benefit to all in the tribe and the 'Beowas' were adopted into their beliefs. It was a phenomenon that could only be explained by the belief of the 'Beowas', for why else would a killer whale home in on a humpback caught in the bay, pester and kill, to feed upon the lips and tongue, and then allow all that which remained to be shored upon the beach in order for the Yuin to feed?

Much else was also sought by the Yuin, not just food and comradely with a whale, but the more in-depth spiritual healing of infliction. It is here that rituals came into existence and all that the killer gave in jester to the people was to be used to full effect. A remedy – so it is said – evolved, where an individual so inflicted with rheumatism and the like would climb into a rotting carcase, naked and up to the neck in blubber, to gain the such sought-after relief gained by spending hours encased within the flesh and absorbing the stench and oil of the baleen's blubber.

1828 – 1830s

Thomas Raine was the first whaler in Twofold Bay in 1828, followed soon after in the 30's by the Imlay Brothers who employed several of the Yuin due to their keen ability to work hard, be reliable, and were easily skilled with the abilities of boat-handling; they were soon recognised for their talent and had good eyesight.

1838

Having sent for his brothers, Dr. Imlay undertook further exploits whereby his interest in breeding cattle continued alongside bay whaling.

1840

And at this time the sperm whale industry took precedence for the humpback whale had become decreasingly available, learning over time to avoid the slaughter that occupied the bays of Tasmania, and although migratory routes were seldom changed and little voiced, it was in the interest of man to hunt where the value of the spoils could be secured in purse, hence the move from one species to the next; although, in all fair response, the sperm whale was also worth more in regards to oil.

1840s

In the 1840s, Benjamin Boyd set upon the scene and commenced to build a town in his own name; Boyd Town. It was his hope to have it grow in all aspects to one day be as big as any other city within Australia. He built a lighthouse from Sydney sandstone on the south head (Boyd's Tower) along with a little church of red brick (the spire of which could be seen from 20 miles out to sea), houses, storage rooms, wharves, stock-yards and the Seashore Inn which is situated on the beach and draws upon the very romance of the area, all surrounded by the lush of eucalyptus trees.

The bush itself was thick and descended to right upon the beach itself. Bay whaling was, however, not something that Boyd took too with great enthusiasm as the competition was so great, so sought to make an ambition from offshore whaling where the sperm whale could still be quarried in large numbers out to sea – for the sperm whale did not frequent the bays or the coast.

His crews were not successful, accusingly bribed by the Imlay Brothers to miss-judge the thrust of a harpoon, but the oil from the sperm whale measured Boyd's greed and filled him to the brim, his ships much more capable of bringing home the oil.

Oswald Briefly, a good friend of Boyd's, who had arrived with him upon his yacht, *Wanderer*, made many written entries within a diary along with paintings and sketches of the activities of men and killer whales alike. It is from these accounts that the first encounter with the killers of Twofold Bay can be found, actually competing against the bay whalers as opposed to helping them, for the crews of bay refused to allow the killers a share and frequently attacked them with the boat spades used in removing blubber from the much sought after baleen. It is here that the first of many strange incidents commences to take shape for the killers begin to show a liking towards those crews less callous in their treatment towards them.

And the men of the crews that fought the whales from upon

their long and sturdy craft took little pity of the killers for their help in the hunt. The men watch as the killer whales fling themselves upon the back of the whale, charge in and takes chunks from its flanks, pester it at every turn in order to prevent it from careering home into the depths of the open sea.

Lances continue to puncture the flesh of the humpback, the first catch in many months, but the fight isn't over just yet, for the whale must be killed and then secured, secured from the lurches of the orca as they come in for the lips and tongue. The crews endeavour to impede the killers' efforts, try with all their might to drag the dead whale away, to be deblubbered at their convenience. This is but one of the many reasons that the killers soon reside to taking their catch whilst near the mouth of the bay as opposed to within it, for the men of Twofold Bay seem to think that the whale is their just reward and should not be shared, and it was only due to the lack of a baleen plates, and little oil to quench the first of the market and merchants, that killers were not rendered into oil.

Twofold Bay was changing face, there was now Eden to the north of the bay and two other small villages, if that, upon the south, separated by the Kiah Inlet. There was Boyd Town to the west and East Boyd to the east.

1843

It had become more than clear, even to those that lived in denial over the growing absence of right whales, that bay whaling in Tasmania was coming to a close. But in lieu of the bay whalers of Twofold Bay the call to boats was made, quite often, with great regularity; not by time of day, but by the appearance of whales from June and on into the long winter months. The sighting of whales in and around Tasmanian bays might have taken a turn for the worst, but the slaughter in and around Twofold Bay had just commenced.

The tides were turning and the great phenomenon was taking shape. Boyd's empire collapsed completely and the whaling gear no longer needed was sold to Alexander W. Davidson and his business partner Solomon Solomon, to sit idle for several years until the boats hit the water.

1849

Boyd departed Australia in 1849.

1895

By 1895 sperm whaling was all but dead and the last unsuccessful hunt on the east coast concluded in 1896.

1955 (Sperm Whale) *Norwegian*

The decline of humpback numbers, not due to the killers themselves, nor even the Davidson's, for the combined number of kills were rather deplorable to say the least; but particular investments such as those of the Norwegians, where whales were taken from Australian waters, certainly aided in the rise of situations within the world such as Frenchman Bay of West Australia taking the turn it did by commencing with sperm whaling and adding infuriation upon a depleted stock.

www.ingramcontent.com/pod-product-compliance
Lightning Source LLC
Chambersburg PA
CBHW050126280326
41933CB00010B/1267